ADVANCING
OUR HUMANNESS...

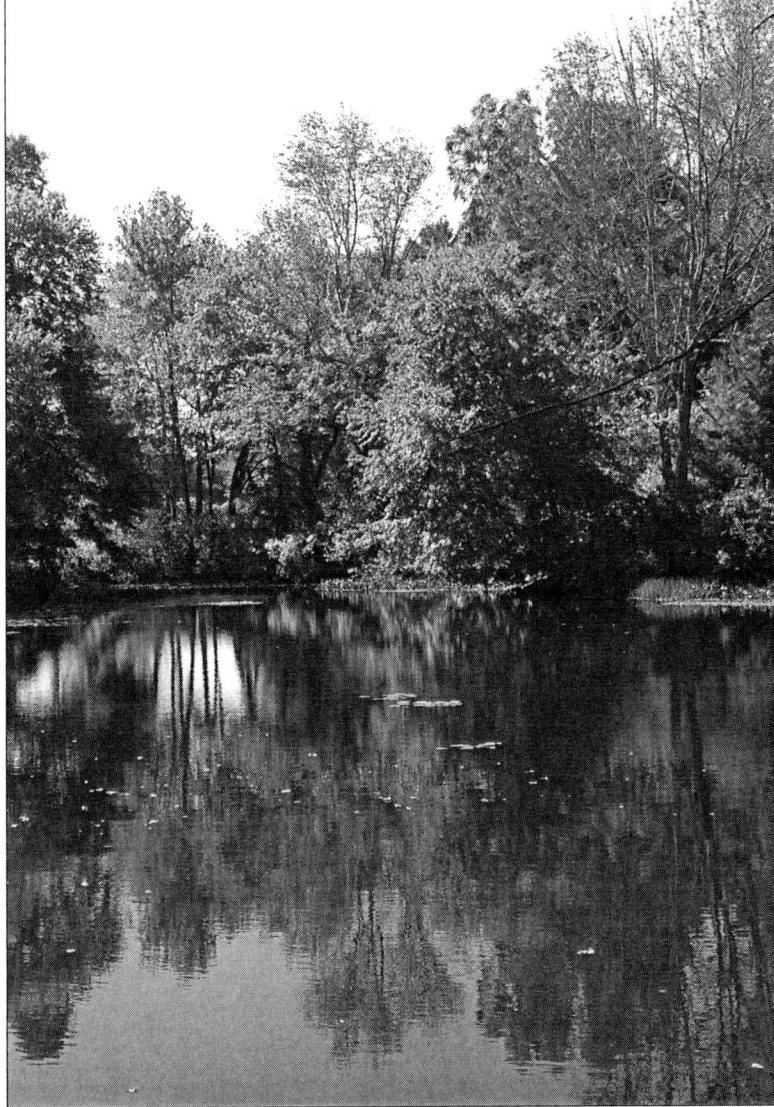

Books from
Path of Potential

The Becoming Intentional People Series:

ADVANCING OUR HUMANNESS... CHOOSING A
PATH OF CONGRUENCE WITH INTENT

INTENTIONAL GRANDMOTHERING... CHOOSING
THE LIFE PHILOSOPHY THAT WORKS FOR ALL
CHILDREN IN THE WORLD

The Desert Series:

WORK FOR ALL CHILDREN

AT THIS TIME OF POTENTIAL

WHO WILL SPEAK FOR EARTH? Reflections on
Securing Energy from a Life of the Whole Perspective

DEVELOPING PLANETARY ETHICS; The Urgent
Work of Today's Generation

Compilations:

GIFTS OF THE SPIRIT; Experiencing Death and Loss
from the Perspective of Potential

Other Writings from Path of Potential
The Path of Potential Library:
www.pathofpotential.org

~

To order books, go to the Path of Potential website, or call:
Melody Fraser, The Mail Suite, 1-800-818-6177 or 1-970-241-8973

ADVANCING OUR HUMANNESS...

Choosing a Path of Congruence with Intent

Terry P Anderson

Path of Potential ™

Advancing our Humanness

PHOTOGRAPHY
Candi Clark
Robin G. Peters
Sandra Maslow Smith

COVER, BOOK DESIGN, and GRAPHICS
Candi Clark

PRINTING
Precision Printing
Grand Junction, CO 81501 • www.ppgj.com

PUBLISHER
Path of Potential
P.O. Box 4058 • Grand Junction, CO 81502 USA
www.pathofpotential.org

AUTHOR
Terry P. Anderson

EDITOR
Sandra Maslow Smith

First printings – 2010-2012
Second printing – 2013
Printed in the United States of America
SFI® Certified (Sustainable Forestry Initiative) Acid Free

ISBN-10: 0-9760139-8-3
ISBN-13: 978-0-9760139-8-3

v

TABLE OF CONTENTS

X

Author's Note...
About The Working of Philosophy

     This book of intent is all about becoming, about our becoming fully and truly human – realizing our potential, fulfilling the original intent of the Source of creation. Realizing our potential requires the accessing of wisdom, the wisdom of intent... the wisdom necessary for taking up our intended work, for living and working in ways congruent with the intention of the Source... work and ways that require us to embrace the truth of our living character – of our being members in the larger community of life.

     This book is philosophy – philosophy of *living* potential. Whether we are conscious of it or not, philosophy – a particular philosophy – is actively present in the principles, concepts, ideals we hold and pursue. This is true regardless of the arena we are part of, or participate within... regardless of whether the arena is government and governance, the practice of our religion, the working of our community, the way we do business, our personal stance, etc.; always behind our thoughts, embedded within, is philosophy – our particular philosophy. It is a bit like a mountain stream that tumbles its way to the valley below – it carries within it the character of its source... that from which it emerges and flows.

     The living philosophy, the life of the whole centered philosophy of potential, carries within it – provides a true taste of – the character of moving towards wholeness, away from that which divides... doing so in ways that work for all children, all children in the world... taking up the work of bringing the world of our making into congruence with the world of original intent, a work that requires a consciousness of intent, of the philosophy that is guiding us and the perspective from which it comes.

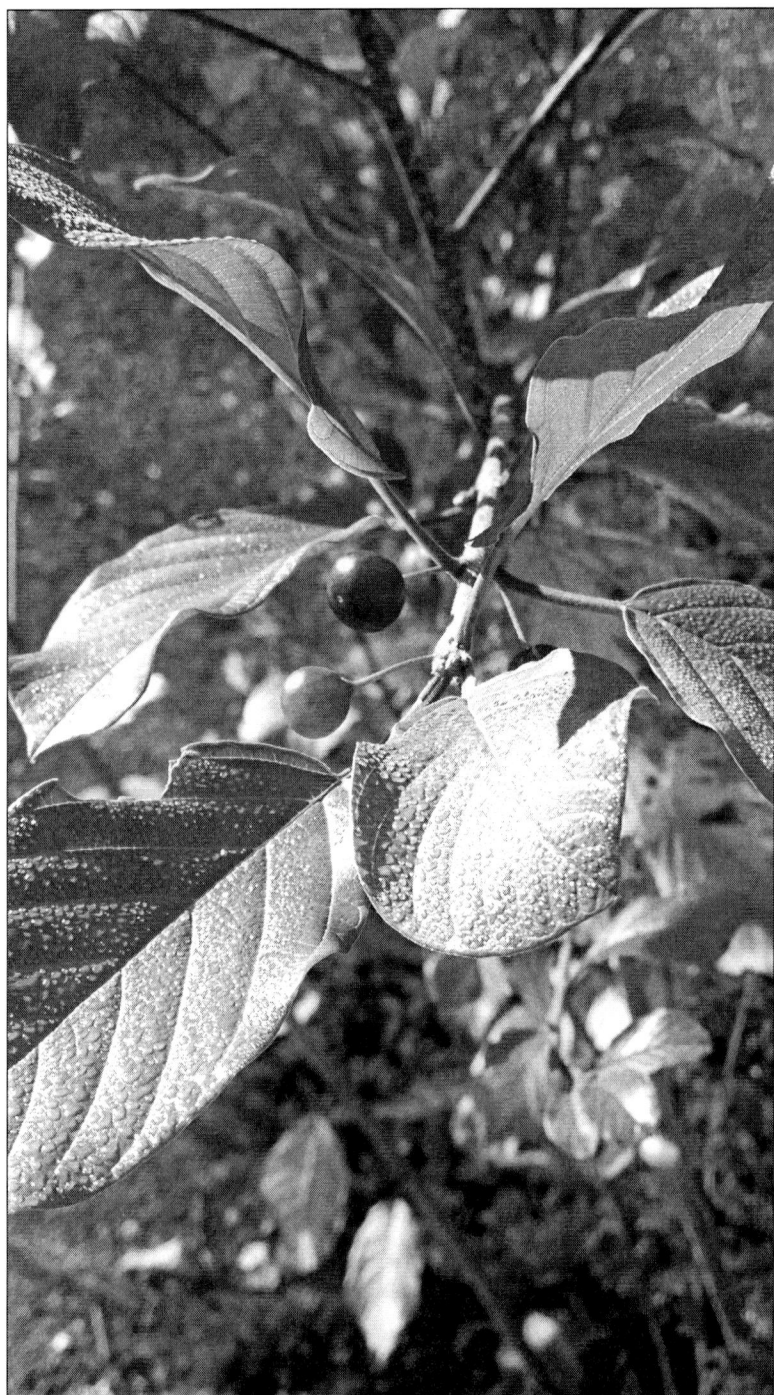

There is among more and more of us, a stirring... an inner recognition of the diminishing of our humanness, and the growing threat to life itself... and through reflection is emerging an increasing clarity of the necessity for shifting the direction and nature of our processes. Humanness, our unique contribution to life, is being called upon to shift upward... to bring about a true advancement... an advancement that becomes possible through serious commitment on our part to take up the unfolded work before us, the work of...

> *Moving towards wholeness, away from that which divides.*
>
> *Taking up pursuits that work for all children, all children in the world.*
>
> *Bringing the world of our making into congruence with the world of intent.*

...work that requires the developing of, and the coming from, a life of the whole perspective... a perspective that embraces the truth of our living nature... the truth of our being, through intent of the Source, members in the larger community of life, the whole of life.

Introduction…

ALL-INCLUSIVE LOVE
AND THE WORK

This Book...

This book, like its partnering companion, Intentional Grandmothering, is all about life... the eternalizing of life on and through earth. This pair, through the intuitive reflective processes of intentional reading and dialoguing, seeks to bring about a coalescence of seeing and understanding with regard to advancing our humanness – our ongoing work in the world... a seeing and understanding of the particular work and initiating roles being called for at this time... the twofold, complementary work of taking up pursuits that work for all children, all children in the world; and bringing the world of our making into congruence with the world of intent. And with regard to that work, taking on the particular initiating roles of creating an active presence of a "work for all children in the world" culture; and of creating the active, path taking, presence of congruence with intent – intended ways of working of life on this earth...

These being the particular work and roles required for the particular advancing humanness work of moving towards wholeness, away from that which divides... from that which artificially, externally segments, separates and divides our human society... and that which, in an illusionary way, separates us from the whole of life... from the Source of life... from our living nature...

Work and roles that require a shift in perspective – moving from a human centered perspective to a life of the whole centered perspective... a perspective that more wholistically embraces original intent, the willful intent out from which emerged and emerges the ongoing living creation...

Work and roles that look to the living philosophy of potential and understand that if all-inclusive love is not present in the process, all-inclusive love will not be present in the outcomes... and that it is the all-inclusive love of the Source entering into the working of the world that makes possible the advancing of our humanness, the ongoingness of life... the particular advancement now being called for... the particular manifestation of unconditioned love... love that we are not the source of, but rather intended instruments... instruments for love's entry.

On Being Certain...
The Going Forward Gift of Certainty

Being certain, an inner sense of certainty, is a welcome and necessary systemic element of our advancing humanness work; innerly experiencing certainty becomes both the grounding source for the spirit and willfulness the work requires, and that which makes visible our path – the intended path, the path of intent. At this time moving towards wholeness away from that which divides is central to our work. Wholeness is the domain of intuition – the intuition of wholeness. Thus it is certainty of intuition – intuitive certainty – that our going forward requires... inner seeing and understanding versus instinctive certainty – the seeking of factual proof, material evidence, etc.

The ongoing reflective processes of intentional reading, writing and dialoguing, inspirited through what we have come to know as prayerful questioning, have brought forth the nature of seeing and understanding that lends itself to intuitive certainty and conscious choice... conscious choice being the nature of choosing that makes an ongoing, authentic "Yes" possible.

To begin with, advancing our humanness is an essence-based, inner evolutionary process... an intrinsically within, upward progression of being and becoming... an inner process versus the externally focused evolution common to science/biological science – the common external, physical and material movement to higher order, more advanced structures and structuring capacity. It is the contrast between the essence-based, intrinsic nature of being and becoming and the existence-based, externally focused progression that has given rise to the expression of "Are we being externally defined or intrinsically expressed?" A simple question which brings forth vivid imagery with regard to

7

path – current path, possible path; and in a similar way with regard to culture – current culture, potential culture: Are we being externally defined by a materially, possessionally, positionally grounded existence-based culture; or intrinsically expressed – enabled by an essence-based culture, an intentional culture… a culture that works for all children in the world?

Advancing our humanness is all about transcending limitations… limitations that are self-imposed… limitations that naturally emerge from the perspectives we hold, philosophies we follow, and the way of working of particular minds – the reasoning mind of existence and the intuitive mind of essence, for example – all of which work to create a particular world view, which in turn greatly influences culture – the culture we create, the cultures we live in, and live under.

The notion of transcending limitations, self-imposed limitations, becomes readily apparent as we reflect on the intentional story of life, and on our life within that. Reflecting on our emergence into the garden of the living earth, we come to see, through the eye of intuition, the working presence of perspective, an intentional perspective with regard to life – life on and through earth. Earth was created for life to have a place to enter into the working of the unfolding creation. Life was at the center. It was/is the central organizing phenomenon of earth. There was clarity with regard to the intended ways of working within life, and with regard to our ways as well. However, a new perspective emerged… a human centered perspective that, through time, became more and more dominant, having dominion over the intentional life perspective that brought forth the living earth and our presence upon it… a human centeredness that through the powers of reason, the discipline of existence-based philosophies, and the gaining and development of

8

manipulative knowledge, continued to move us in a direction away from original intent... away from the perspective that honored our livingness, our intended ways of living, of being and doing, within the garden of life. Our thinking, our pursuits, our behaviors were more and more a reflection of self... of our human self... a self-centeredness that enabled our seeing of ourselves as separate from life... a self-centeredness that gave rise to notions of earth having been created for man – man's dominance, man's pleasure, man's disposal... a human centeredness, a self-centeredness, that required an intervention... an intervention aimed at saving us, saving us from ourselves, from our self-centeredness... an intervention that would turn us towards, begin our return to, the path of intent... turn us away from self-love and towards being and becoming instruments for love – the unconditioned love of the Source – entering into the working of the world... turn us away from the instinctive, the materialities of existence; and move us towards the intuitive, the building of soul, the manifesting of spirit... soul building and spirit manifesting being the very essence of our work on this earth, that which reciprocally nourishes the Source and enables the ongoing upward unfolding of life.

One of the beauties of life is its wholistic and systemic way of working... a way of being and working that often becomes invisible to that which we are focused on... fully present – like water is to the fish – but not actively present within our awareness. And too, that which we are focused upon can, through a bit of reflection, be seen as an inevitable manifestation of our system of thought – perspective, philosophy, the particular mind engaged, for example. As such we can see the external focus, our being externally defined, as a natural manifestation of our human centered, existence-based ways and culture; we can see the ensuing limitations, pursuits and behaviors, and the issues that emerge with regard to instinct and space – positional space,

9

possessional space, accessing and exercising rights, etc. – that, given the dominance of the reasoning mind of existence, become problems to solve... giving way to seeking solutions that commonly follow a path of legality, albeit a morally energized path, but a path of legality nonetheless.

One of the more visible manifestations of external focus, of our being externally defined, of our being subject to artificial boundaries and imposed limitations, is that of color of skin and gender... boundaries and limitations that are seen and sustained by the eye of the reasoning mind of existence... an eye that, even in the presence of imposed legality, morally energized laws, continues its influential, external focus... an eye not belonging to one color, one gender, but rather one actively present within all colors, all genders... a separating self-focused eye... the eye that we wish would become blind – blind to color, blind to gender... an eye we wish would see beyond color... to character, to potential. Yet, an eye, to which there is much attachment.

We have come to see that the particular advancement of our humanness being called for requires a shift, a true shift in perspective, a shift towards and to a life of the whole perspective... a perspective that moves us in the direction of being and becoming an intentional people, a people moving along the path of intent, moving towards being and becoming fully and truly human... a perspective shift that requires an essence-based philosophy – the living philosophy of potential – and the development of the intuitive mind of essence, the emergence of an eye that sees essence – patterns of intent – and focuses on the intrinsic versus the external... an eye that can see the path, the way, the working of a culture that works for all children, all my children in the world... transcending the limitations of skin color and gender through pursuits that work for all children in the world – pursuits that enable the building of soul, the

10

manifesting of spirit… not a blind eye, but an eye that can see and lead the process, the currently necessary process, of advancing our humanness.

Perhaps, with regard to our developing a deeper sense of certainty, nothing is more helpful than the understanding that the essence of the truths of the previous are not discarded or lost; but rather are enfolded within the upward unfolding, and re-emerge as deeper, more wholistic, expressions of truth… a reassuring reality, but one requiring faith, much faith, going forward faith on our part.

We can see this pattern at work through reflecting on the unfolding path of love… the unconditioned love of the Source… love entering into the working of the world, its influential trace entwined within the intentional story of life… within and from the Life, the unfolding life on earth…

Within ourselves we can see an intended unfolding… an upward unfolding of love… of our moving from highly conditioned love towards unconditioned love. We see the instinctive love of self, for one's own, one's family, one's tribe… for that which relates to blood lineage. We can see the truth of that being enfolded into love of neighbor, the intent for us to *love our neighbor as our self* (Mk12:31)… and the truth of that being enfolded into the intent for us to *love one another as I have loved you* (Jn13:34), a love, an inclusive love, that transcends blood lineage, an all-inclusive love entering into the world that moves us along the path of intent… towards the unconditioned love of the Source… and our becoming instruments for that – the all-inclusive love… the all-inclusive love that makes possible both a work for all children in the world culture and the bringing of the world of our making into congruence with the world of intent. The former making possible the building of the soul of the human community, with the latter making possible the taking up of manifesting spirit work – working and living in ways congruent with intent, the intended ways of working of life on earth.

Advancing our humanness is an essence-based, virtue sourced, value adding process... a process that acknowledges both the realities and necessities of life and intent – original and unfolding intent – through the development of reciprocally nourishing economics around that, around the essence-based, virtue sourced, value adding process... reciprocally nourishing economics that enable soul building and manifesting spirit. With a bit of reflection on our long history, or just by looking about us, we can see the inevitable diminishment of humanness when we start our process – our thinking, our pursuits – with economics. An inevitable reality regardless of the person, the community, the business, the institution, the country, etc. We both see and know from experience, the soul selling, spirit diminishing path... a more material and self-serving path... a path wherein purpose and meaning are overshadowed by power, control, leveraged advantage for the few... a divisive path, a path of anger – not love – and coarse energies... a path truly incongruent with a path of intent, incongruent with a true path of our potential.

Returning, in a closing way, to certainty, that which we are certain of...

> *We are not the Source.*

> *There is a Source, a will force, an intentional way of working of life on this earth.*

> *The true hierarchy is a hierarchy of One: One Source; all else equal – developable instruments of the*

intended unfolding.

> *We, through congruence with intent, have the potential to be co-creators… an intentional people… an intrinsically expressed, soul building, spirit manifesting people.*

And finally,

> *A path that seeks to create the active presence of a work for all children in the world culture; seeks to create an active, path-taking presence of congruence with intent; a path where the truths of the previous, the current, can emerge as intentional ethics – right for humanity, good for the whole of life ethics; is without doubt a path of hope, hope for each, hope for all… a realizable hope in that through love, the love of the Source, all things are possible.*

The first of this three volume work is all about taking up the path of intent, the path of our potential... a way of moving away from, transcending the limitations of the perspective expressed in "We are only human, restrained and constricted by our sinful nature"... and moving towards becoming fully and truly human... realizing the potential made possible through the spirit manifesting process of Christ... always remembering a spirit manifested is available forever and to all – to all of life.

Volume One...

TAKING UP THE PATH
OF INTENT

*Bringing the World of our Making into
Congruence with the World of Intent*

The Questioning Path in Search of Truth

The questioning path I first stepped upon as I rounded the bend from Unstrahle's Hole on the West Branch Creek has finally led me to "the top of the mountain" – a seeing and understanding that is expressed in the words, "taking up the path of intent." It is an interesting thing about truth, that once you see it, it is seemingly so obvious. Perhaps the trick is to sustain the upward climb required to develop the mind – the eye – that can see, and the ear – the inner ear – that can hear. For me this has been a lifelong struggle. And I am sure there are – and you will discover – higher mountains; but this, for me at least, seems to be the top of the mountain.

Some of the most obvious truths – perhaps a bit unsettling – are:

One Source; all – everything else – instruments.

Earth was created for life to have a place to enter into the working of the universe. We, as living human beings are – not accidentally, but intentionally – created as members in the larger community of life. Thus it and everything is all about life – our role, our work within that.

Original intent preceded – came before – original sin, our fall from grace and the unintended path of salvation.

If love is not present in the process, love will not be present in the outcomes.

As I write this note, I am remembering and revisiting my first real question, wondering as to whether or not there was a God, and recalling the imagery and understanding that emerged – after quite a bit of time – in that regard. Now,

17

after all these years, those first impressions still bear much truth for me. But then that is another story.

Better that I close for now. In closing, these essential truths regarding our essential work as living human beings come to mind:

Building, purifying soul.
Manifesting spirit.

Of course there still is the matter of existence – sustaining and maintaining existence, our existence. The trick here is to have our essential work and the requirements of existence be so interwoven that they become one and the same.

Terry P. Anderson
July, 2010

Perpetual Intent

Intent is actively present...
      continuously at work in the whole of creation.

Wisdom is present to intent;
      Wisdom sees and understands
            intended ways of working – the truths of intent.

Ever since the beginning, the beginning of the process through which life emerged on earth, there has been intent, intent manifested through intended ways of working: intended ways of working of the living system we know as earth, intended ways of working for the whole of life, and for life's members – including ourselves as living human beings.

What is most obvious in this living world of intent is that we are not the source. What is equally obvious, after a bit of reflective seeing and understanding, is that we – like other communities of life – are intended to be instruments, instruments that have real work and roles to carry out.

The wisdom of intent is accessible; the seeing and understanding of intent is accessible through the intuition of wholeness. This is good news, not only for ourselves, but for the whole of life on earth. This makes it possible for our path to be one not of stumbling and haphazard experimentation, but rather one of seeing and understanding... a path and a way of living and working more congruent with the intent of the Source... a path whereby we and life can fulfill our purpose – our reason for being on earth.

This path of intent, this path of our potential to become fully and truly human, is a path we seem to have a habit of wandering away from, wanderings that share some common points of departure, the most common seeming to be the loss of faith and trust in the Source – the intentional Source – a loss often accompanied by illusionary efforts to establish ourselves as the source, or to establish that which we construct as the source. We see this at work in the various creation stories of earth's people, an apparent willful forgetting that all – all on earth – are instruments, instruments through which truth, love and good can enter into the working of the world, but instruments nevertheless. There is but one Source. Clear understanding of Source and instrument is critical to our staying on path.

Wisdom of Intent, and Reason

Ever since our first wandering off the path of intent, we have been "encouraged," whether through experience or intervention, to bring the world of our making into congruence with the world of intent – with intended ways of working. As we look about our world of today – at what we are experiencing, in particular with regards to the children – the urgent need for bringing about congruence between the world of our making and the world of intent is blatantly obvious to more and more of us. What perhaps is less obvious – given the culture we swim in – is the process of going forth. An operating element of any culture is status, that which we give status to. Status is often thought of as the ground, the very basis for a culture and its working, a real point of orientation for the people – what we pay attention to, the focal point of our effort and energy. We who live in this culture are all too familiar with the status of stuff, and the stuff we give status to. Elaboration on this is neither necessary nor within the scope of this writing. What is well within the scope of this writing, however, is the understanding that if we are serious, truly serious about shifting the ground – the platform upon which we live and work – we must begin with the wisdom of intent, the wisdom required to guide reason such that the intents of reason – our intents – can move towards being more and more congruent with the intent of the Source.

Wisdom is what we seek, to see the whole of something, to see and understand its intended way of working. It is what we look to when our aim is in regards to realizing potential, to our becoming. Reason's domain is problem and problem-solving. It tends to move away from wholeness towards fractionation and reduction. In a way, it thrives in the domain of material and the energies of existence.

When the wisdom of intent drops out, we, through reason and reasoned interpretation, commonly shape our existence – our ways of living and working – in accord with our image, our intents, our desires. And inevitably, as our intents grow increasingly out of tune with "the intent," we become more self-focused, more self-serving; ultimately we move further away from our instrumentality and more towards the illusion of our being the source – in many ways, seeing ourselves as the source of/in control of life.

Through the gift of reason, we have a capacity for understanding, creating and building structures. In the absence of the wisdom of intent, that which we create does not bring spirit and meaning into existence, into our life, but rather turns this gift of reason against us, against the whole of life.

Unfolding Intent

Unfolding is a natural process within life... a seed unfolds into a flower, a fertilized egg unfolds into one of life's creatures, a sand dune, first covered with simple organisms, becomes home to increasingly complex living structures and systems. Inherent within this unfolding are processes and cycles... processes which sustain the active presence of life, and cycles within which particular unfoldings occur. Seemingly present within this unfolding is a will force... a will to live, to struggle, to survive, to grow, to develop, to procreate – to bring into existence offspring of one's own kind, to enable their growth, development...

There is an unfolding within the processes and cycles of life, and then – from time to time – unfoldings that represent step changes, real shifts in life's platforms. Looking at life from the perspective of existence – in material and energy terms – we tend to see structure, a kind of thingness. We see progressions in structure and in complexity of structure. When structural progressions represent step changes, we often think of these as being evolutionary in character. For example, we could look at the structural shifts present in ableness to fly, versus those present in walking, as being evolutionary. In a very real sort of way, this view of evolution is an external point of view, one that focuses on the material – the physical and energetic – manifestations of life... manifestations which draw the attention of reason, for this is the natural workplace of reason. Now the actions of reason – the compartmentalization, segmentation, fractionation, the gaining of knowledge, discovery, experimentation, manipulation, etc., actions of reason – spring to life. And as reason seeks to advance its knowledge, theories emerge – theories being instruments critical to the ongoing advancement of knowledge... theories aimed at completeness, a more complete explanation of the observed, the physically observable... theories themselves which experience evolutionary shifts – step changes in knowledge. What does not change, however, is the perpetual truth of Source: there is a Source beyond ourselves; we are not the source.

As stated in the beginning, the focus of our writing is becoming... becoming fully and truly human... becoming an intentional people. Becoming much more relates to being, than to the physical, the material, the things of existence. When it comes to being, our attention shifts from the external, from knowledge and knowing about ourselves, to the intrinsic, to intrinsic expressions and manifestations... a real shift from being externally, culturally defined to being intrinsically expressed... a shift that turns us towards spirit, towards the accessing and manifesting of spirit. We look to the seeing and understanding of wholistic truths versus gaining knowledge regarding the factual basis of existence. Essence, the pattern of intent, comes to the fore. It is the seeing and understanding of essential truths, and the coming from essence that is critical to advancing our being... critical to the process by which we move towards oneness with the intent of the Source, to our becoming more fully and truly human. Thus we need to turn our attention to, and seek the wisdom of intent.

Evolutionary, upward shifts along the path of our becoming are not unfamiliar to us. We see this at work in the reflective experience – the intrinsic historical experience – of the people of earth. Various communities of earth's people have their own particularlized remembrance, but a common pattern seems to be present. There is a clear shift in the ground or platform upon which to live and work... a move from one world to the next world – the next advancement. An upward shift in potential and expectation is introduced – made accessible and present... potential to be realized, expectations regarding how we are to relate one to another – between and among communities of life. And frequently, the people bring into this new world some attachments – structural and structuring elements of the previous world – that are not necessarily needed or perhaps not intended to be carried across this threshold, but nevertheless are brought along.

We can look at the Christ impulse – the entry of Christ, physically and spiritually, into the working of the world – as an intended unfolding… an upward shift, a true step change along the path of our becoming… an intended unfolding that brought (brings) spirit and life to two particular urges, urges held deep within us: our longing to return, our yearning to become. And, as well, brought spirit, life and hope to a people who had been disconnected from the Source – from returning to the Source… to a people who awaited the fulfillment of prophetic predictions.

The earliest unfolding of this shift – of new expectations and potential – centered around reconnection and return – salvation, of being saved. Not surprising given the realities of the time, the realities of the people. What began as a process organized around a core of salvation – of being saved – eventually became more structured, more formalized through the establishment of a religion… a religion organized around the teachings of Christ… a religion that included the manifested word of God that preceded Christ's entry into the world. Through time, through the work of reasoned interpretation, theologies were developed… theologies which sought to explain what was meant by God's words and the teachings of Christ. In one sense, an effort to make clear what the people were expected to know, expected to do, expected to be obedient to… an effort leaning more towards expectations than potential; much more focused on salvation than becoming… with a resultant focusing on human weaknesses and failings versus human potential – our potential to become fully and truly human, the potential that is the force, the will force, behind our urge to become, the source of our calling to be and become.

Which brings us back to becoming, the particular becoming being called for at this time… a becoming that authentically encompasses the realities of now, and clearly enables our advancement – the advancement of our being and becoming fully and truly human. To this end, we turn to the essence of becoming: our moving towards oneness with the intent of the Source… a oneness made possible by the path and way opened up through the impulse of Christ… a way made visible through the absolute clarity regarding Source and instrument, perhaps first made visible through Mary's "Yes" – a conscious yes, a conscious choice on her part… a yes to instrumentality firmly secured by Christ's surrendering to the will, the intent of the Father.

Thus the way, our way if we are to follow this established path, also begins with a yes… a conscious choice, not a pattern that emanates from tradition, habit or heritage, but rather an authentic yes, a surrendering on our part… a way further clarified through the teachings, the philosophy, the principles, the going forward gospels of Christ… a way, a path of intent, requiring our accessing the wisdom of intent. For the wisdom of intent – if we are open and receptive – will provide the seeing and understanding that will lead us, show us the path of our moving towards oneness with the intent of the Source. This seeing and understanding which comes about through the intuition of wholeness does not in any way diminish the work and role of reason, for reason has much work to do both in terms of actualizing and realizing the intent at this time of potential, a time of moving towards wholeness, away from that which divides – wholeness being the domain of intuition and wisdom. It is a time for bringing the world of our making into congruence with the world of intent – the intended unfolding made possible through the entry of Christ into the working of the world… an entry made whole and authentic through the willful completion of his work on earth, his fulfilling of the intent of the Source, a fulfillment that returned, reopened for us the path of intent – the path of our potential.

It is the fulfillment of Christ's work that leads the way, that makes possible our taking up our intended work, the work of our calling – the work called for at this time of potential… working not so much as individuals, but as gatherings of two or more, as communities, as a community of humankind – members of the larger community of life. It is in the acceptance of the intentionality of our living nature – our membership in the whole of life – that we are able to transcend our human centeredness and enter into this cycle of becoming with a life of the whole perspective… a perspective that allows us to be authentic instruments in the light of the realities of now… a perspective that enables our moving towards oneness with the intent of the Source… a perspective that enables us to pursue wholistic, life of the whole approaches; and one that helps ensure that what we pursue will work for all children, all children in the world.

This path is not a path of our making, rather a path prepared for our taking. Thus a path for courage, not fear. With a prepared path awaiting us, we can go forward with hope – genuine, authentic hope. For hope always has, and always will lie upon and along the path of intent… a path not of our making, a path for our taking… a path of "Yes."

Essence of Teachings

Christ, having completed his work, left with us that which we would need to go forward along our intended path.

Our way of praying...

> *Our Father, who art in heaven, hallowed be thy name; thy kingdom come, thy will be done on earth...*

Three principles/commandments...

> *Love God.* (MK12:30)

> *Love one another as I have loved you,* (JN13:34)

> *The Father's command is eternal life... on earth as in heaven* (JN12:50; MT6:10).

> What greater glory would Christ experience before the Father than our bringing the world of our making into congruence with the world of intent... our choicefully, willfully moving towards oneness with the intent of the Source, our becoming intentional beings?

The going forward gospels...

> Seeing and understanding the essence of these teachings through reflection and reflective dialogue aimed at accessing the wisdom of intent... a process requiring a perspective of potential and the intuition of wholeness.

Keeping on the Path of Intent

Intent is actively present...
continuously at work in the whole of creation.

Wisdom is present to intent;
Wisdom sees and understands
intended ways of working – the truths of intent.

There is intent, intentionality behind the whole of creation... intent as will, a will force behind, and emanating from the Source... a will force intentionally establishing a particular relatedness between Source and all: There is but one Source; with all – the whole of life and its members – being instruments. There is an intended relatedness, "relatedness" (versus relationship) in that this term lifts up for us the systemic interaction between Thy will, my intended work, and intended ways of working. We see the relatedness of Source and instrument at work in the words of Christ, *Thy will* (not my will) *be done on this earth* (MT6:10). Wisdom is present to intent, sees and understands intended unfolding, a seeing and understanding that is accessible through the intuition of wholeness. Thus making it possible for us to honor this intention of will – to be and become instruments. It is our having this ultimate truth actively present in heart and mind that both enables and makes possible our keeping on the path of intent. (MT6:10).

Reflective seeing in regards to our keeping on the path of intent is aided by a bit of imaging of mind and its way of working. Most simply, at essence, mind is an organizing process (versus structure; structure of the brain, for example). We can see mind at work through our witnessing of the swarming of bees, through our witnessing of the synchronous flying of an endless flock of blackbirds; witnessing in the sense of our being open to and appreciating the mystery, the wonder, the beauty and the awe of what is before us (versus the reductive closing of analysis, for example).

Reflecting wholistically on mind, we can see two distinct, but complementary – each completing the other – organizing processes. One being the mind of existence, the other being the mind of essence; one anchoring itself in existence, the other in essence; both having intentional purposes, intended work. Both – with right orientation/relatedness – enable our bringing the world of our making into congruence with the world of intent.

The mind of existence – the organizing process of reason – needs structure to have meaning… structures and structuring not limited to the physical and material, but including such things as relationships, words, etc. A need that is more satisfied through naming. We can gain a bit of seeing in this regard by imaging ourselves walking through a woodland and observing within ourselves, the hearing of a sound… and our being (or perhaps not being) able to say/to know that the sound comes from a bird… that bird being a chickadee; the sound we are hearing being its mating call. And further, we might notice that often (particularly when interacting with nonhuman entities) we personify; we give it characteristics, create thoughts about it, that make it more like us – humanize it so to speak… a personifying process often aimed at building a relationship – a seemingly closer bond between it and us… an energizing process, with energies such as liveliness, renewing, excitement and interest becoming more available and accessible to us… energies we often experience between one another as human beings.

The mind of essence – the organizing process of wisdom – looks to spirit and process – the seeing and understanding of process… the processes of unfolding, of seeing and coming from essence... processes of intent, the accessing of the wisdom of intent – seeing intended unfolding. We can get a glimpse of its working by reflecting on an experience common to many: considering, designing, acquiring, building, remodeling a house for self, family, friends... a home for us. Often, herein, is an imaging of processes, processes related to intended ways of working of the house, processes such as preparing a meal, the sharing of a meal, the welcoming and engaging of friends, etc.... a seeing of processes that form the structuring – mindful structuring that guides the creation of the structures we commonly refer to as the kitchen, family room, dining area, great room, etc.... structures that enable the living out of the virtues and values we intend and hope for, virtues and values aimed at enriching and inspiriting – drawing spirit into – our way of life... structures that enable our way of developing, our way of being and becoming; that which can bring about for us, and others as well, a real sense of home, of being at home, a life sustaining, a life renewing sense of home.

Reflecting further, we can begin to see the wholistic complementary working of these minds. First off we can see both the naturalness and necessity for structures and structuring such as food, housing, clothing, relationship, etc. All of which seem to be essential for sustaining our existence – our very presence on earth... requirements not only for ourselves, but seemingly common to other members of life as well. Likewise we can see the significance and sense of purpose that enters the seeing of and coming from essence... and the inner realness we experience through the accessing and manifesting of spirit. We can, with a bit of effort, differentiate – distinguish between – essence and existence, between spirit and material, between process and structure. And at times we can experience the division within ourselves, of our being drawn towards one or the other, often wishing for/seeking for both. It is intent that enables us to transcend that which divides, to realize wholeness, to experience the complementary working of essence and existence – to experience the intentional mind at work, the intentional mind being the mind of wisdom guiding the mind of reason working as a complementary whole. It is the accessing of the wisdom of intent that enables seeing processes, processes for guiding our structuring and structures with intended ways of working on earth, ways acknowledging and honoring our membership in the whole of life. With right orientation, with intended relatedness; with the minds of essence and existence working wholistically – working intentionally – thus allowing spirit to enter into existence; with the daily nourishment of spirit necessary for advancing our humanness, our becoming fully and truly human; with spirit entering as a manifestation of will, the will of intent; the necessities of existence – that which we pursue – will be and become truer reflections of intent, of Thy will, not my will.

Returning to the work of keeping on the path of intent, a few thoughts emerge. The first and most critical is never losing site of the ultimate truth: One Source; all else instruments. Other thoughts emerge related to hazards along this path – hazards viewed more appropriately as temptations, temptations that turn us away from the Source; that lead us off of the path of intent.

One such hazardous temptation shows up in the structures and structuring we create around intentional processes. We can see this at work in structures, hierarchical structures, institutions, etc., that we have formed and brought into existence. It is quite natural for those involved and associated with such to develop through time a real sense of ownership and identity with the structure. Hazard creeps in when we begin to see the structure as all-important... seeing and treating it as more important than the intentional process and purpose around which it formed, which through time disenables its intended work, its intended way of working; thus ultimately the structure/structuring losing its relevance, its reason to exist.

Another temptation can show up in the gaining of knowledge and expertise regarding structures and structuring. As our capacity to create and manipulate structures increases, we can be led along a path that blinds us to intended ways of working... a path that turns us more towards our will, towards ourselves, with lessening regard for the whole of life, and diminishing consideration of ultimate consequences to the ongoingness of life itself.

A third temptation relates to our natural (perhaps habitual) inclination to personify – to impart human characteristics – to the nonhuman. We see this in the world of existence – both with living and that which we consider inanimate. We also see it in regards to the Source. Here the humanizing process introduces the hazard of obscuring will, obscuring the intent and intended relatedness of Source and instrument; an intended relatedness that is quite apparent in this excerpt from the going forward gospels:

JESUS SAID TO HIS DISCIPLES: *This is my commandment: Love one another as I love you. No one has greater love than this, to lay down one's life for one's friends. You are my friends, if you do what I command you* (JN15:12-14).

Finally, we have mentioned heart and mind, but written mostly about mind. Thus a thought or two about heart to complete this writing. Openness, as it is with the mind, is essential to the working of the heart... in particular, openness to love entering. The essence of our instrumentality is for us to be and become instruments for love entering into the working of the world. Given that, it is critical that we

33

have some understanding of openness of heart – processes in that regard. The process that comes to mind is that of forgiveness, forgiveness that opens the heart to love entering, to spirit dwelling within, and manifestation of both. Now forgiveness is not about forgetting – striving to put the offence out of existence. But there does seem to be a need for, a real sense of, "turning it loose," letting go such that we – through hate and anger – are not blocking love entering. Now life experience tells us that, that which we turn loose can return, not just once, but again, and perhaps again and again. The hope here lies in that its returning serves to awaken us to the necessity for heart to be open – open to love entering – reminding us of the necessity for our consciously choosing an organizing process of love versus being receptive to the common, often habitual process of anger and hate.

Anger and hate come to us and through us from existence. Existence is the common source of both – and both are of this world. They are instruments the world uses to be our master – to cause us to be a slave of existence, a slave of the world.

It seems it would be uncommon, perhaps impossible in its purest form, for either hate or anger to enter through essence. This thought produces a glimpse of the intentional purpose of the Christ impulse – the *intentional why* of Christ coming to earth, coming into existence... a coming into existence that carried with it the real possibility of his being "captured," of his becoming of this world, rather than of the Father who sent him. The glimpse of the *intentional why: to make real our potential to escape the slavery of this world – neither being mastered by it, nor seeking to be master of it...* both of which honor and pursue false images – images of our making, not of the intent and unfolding image of the Source... a potential made real by his fulfillment of intent

– completing his work – and the manifestation of Spirit which followed… a Spirit forever present and available to all… all of which leads to seeing the *intentional what* of Christ being related to returning, our returning to the Source, a process we often think of or name as salvation, as being saved, and the *intentional why* of Christ being related to becoming, our becoming fully and truly human, becoming intentional beings; ultimately becoming an intentional people of earth.

Relatedness and Relationship

JESUS SAID TO HIS DISCIPLES: *This is my commandment: love one another as I love you. No one has greater love than this, to lay down one's life for one's friends. You are my friends if you do what I command you. I no longer call you slaves, because a slave does not know what his master is doing. I have called you friends, because I have told you everything I have heard from my Father. It was not you who chose me, but I who chose you and appointed you to go and bear fruit that will remain, so that whatever you ask the Father in my name he may give you. This I command you: love one another* (JN15:12-17, The New American Bible).

...You are my friends – we have a relationship... if you do what I command you – if you maintain right *relatedness* to me.

...Such a beautiful and clear articulation of intent, and the intended way of working of relatedness and relationship... a perfect reflection of the truth and realness of Source and instrument at work: If you do as I command, I will call you friend, a friend for whom one could lay down his life, called and considered a friend, not a slave... an articulation that becomes more whole, more complete, as we bring into our imagery the two commandments: *Love God* (MK12:30) and *Love one another as I have loved you* (JN13:34).

Relationship is about energy – energies of interaction, sharing of energies, energizing, being energized, etc. Relatedness is about will, the will in regard to the working and integrity of living systems: the will behind the system, the will demanded of the systemic elements, and will coalesced by intentional purpose. Relationship, being concerned with energies, is active – present in existence, in life experience, often involves arrangements of multiple components to create a particular effect (a material systemic-ness), and can operate from and within existence. Relatedness is about spirit, spirit entering, spirit entering through essence into existence. Now, when relationship is sourced in spirit – unfolds from/out of relatedness – the life energies possible are at a different level than that accessible through existence. Thus, the act of faith.

Common to us is to "value" relationships such that we will not risk disturbing them by anchoring in spirit. We become guarded, not surrendering to intent; rather seeking to sustain the energizing interactions (often accompanied by a sense of security, comfort with what is) currently present to us. Yet, the truth of the matter is spirit-sourced relationships surely are beyond any relationships possible through existence energies. Thus the real risk is not to experience life in the spirit... a notion that gets us closer to seeing *the Life* referred to in: *I am the way, the truth, and the life* (JN14:6).

Instrumentality requires a shedding of identifications, identifications with current ways of structuring – putting aside present identifications and attachments, identifications with structures such as religion, science, business, governance, etc., and attachment to current structuring of roles such as wife, mother, husband, father, etc., putting all of that aside in the surrendering to instrumentality – saying "Yes" – which allows spirit to enter and become the Source, the enlightening Source for identifications, roles, etc. – putting them on a new plane, a spirit-sourced plane. All of which requires our taking up the path of intent... and keeping on the path.

For example, if we are coming solely from the mind of existence, not led by relatedness, we see that relationship and feelings are to the feminine what logic and facts are to the masculine. It was relationships and feelings that Mary had to transcend to gain a right orientation to relatedness/will – the relatedness of herself to the will of God. Once this was established – surrendered to – the willful spirit-sourced relationships with husband, etc., emerged – relationships of depth and love not otherwise possible; but not automatically achieved, there being some real hazard and risk here. The "friend gospel" of Christ beautifully states this when he says, *You are my friends, if you do as I command you,* saying you will be friend, not slave, but you still are required to do as I command you. All of existence, even that which we experience as good, comes from, is intended to be led by, the ultimate truth of relatedness. Thus friendship/marriage, etc., is only truly working when it does not inhibit relatedness, our relatedness to the will of the Source; and only become true when relatedness is actively present. Embracing this truth is what makes one's intent become a serious intent.

Will and Motivation

Bringing the world of our making into congruence with the world of intent... pursuing life of the whole approaches that work for all children in the world... being accountable for structures that we bring into existence – into the world... creating a better living world for our children... all call upon will.

Will, as we understand, is quite different from motivation. Will is drawn into us and through us; motivation is something we can self-generate or perhaps have externally imposed on us. Motivation is most often about goals, and goals relate to existence. Goals allow a narrow focus, narrow in that they allow us to ignore – be blind to – much of that which surrounds the goal. Will, on the other hand, opens us up to the whole and the intended working of the whole. It is not uncommon to see motivation and goal-focus obscure important, significant realities... obscure such that there is a void, a lack of concern, in regards to any real value being present to humanity, or attention to serious consequences to life.

For example, the motivation of science/scientist is discovery; the essence of science is understanding structure, structuring at interfaces. In the presence of will, the focus shifts to understanding intended ways of working (versus imposing our desires upon it) and in the process, lifting up for all a real sense of awe and beauty in regard to what is before us... and it maintains a conscious eye towards what we have the capacity to manage. Thus avoiding the "outrunning of our headlights" that is so common today.

Thus we see that those whose aim is related to right and good, ethical ways – keeping in mind the children and the life of the whole – look to will, the will of intent, intended ways of working. Motivational energies can then be shaped and led towards intentional outcomes. Questions and questioning imagery seem to be useful to awaken will, such that we are not being driven by blind motivation. Perhaps some starting point for generating these would be questions such as:

> What is the destiny of this path, the obvious end point?
>
> Where is the better life for all children?
>
> What is the value of this to people, to all people, to life, to all life?

Going Forward Thoughts

As we go forward, we are...

> *Always remembering that ultimately the perspective we hold determines*

>> *the path we walk upon,*

>> *the way we live and work along that path,*

>> *and the thinking, behaving and doing we engage in...*

And of course, we are...

> *Paying particular attention to process...*

>> *Faith as Process*

>> *Hope as Process*

>> *Love as Process*

> *as it was in the beginning...*

Faith as Process

Faith as process is having faith in the intent of the Source, a faith that can be manifested and lived out as trust... trust in the intent, the wholistic intent of the Source... trust that enables our congruency with intended ways of working.

A common experience of faith, perhaps not unexpected given the path we have been on, comes to us through the constructs of "my faith", "your faith", "our faith"... constructs that provide a centering force for ourselves; ones that we can take identity from and can develop a sense of ownership of, an identity and ownership that serve to differentiate ourselves from others/the faith of others... a distinctive and meaningful difference even in the presence of coming from a common Source... differences considered to be so significant that serious effort to maintain separation is common.

Now is the time of potential... a time for moving towards wholeness, away from that which divides... a wholeness that embraces and seeks to synthesize the essential truths of the word, the works, and a life of the whole perspective... a real step change, an unfolding that enables us to live out and from our purpose for being here, to fulfill the intent of the Source.

Ownership and identity are natural progressions towards purpose, towards being and becoming purposeful, but they can become attachments – true temptations – that keep us from moving towards purpose, towards intentional purpose which always involves larger wholes, wholes larger than we currently serve. We can see this at work in the call to move towards wholeness, away from that which divides, in ways that work for all children, all children in the world. Which brings us back to faith, the process of faith out from which an authentic yes, a yes to instrumentality, can emerge... a yes not free of discomfort, but a necessary yes to sustain this process of becoming – of our moving towards oneness with the intent of the Source, towards becoming fully and truly human... the process initiated and made possible through some authentic yeses many years ago (LK1:38, 22:42).

And so as we work to create that which will enable our centering in the larger whole called for at this time, perhaps some understanding – understanding of the working of unfolding – will bring welcome reassurance to us. In unfoldings such as this, the essential truths of the previous are not discarded, but rather are enfolded into the unfolding... emerging with more depth, more beauty, more potential. We can see this at work in the teachings of Christ, and in his articulation of what we know as the two commandments – the going forward principles, *Love God* (MK12:30) and *Love one another as I have loved you* (JN13:34): Through reflection we notice seeking salvation leans a bit towards oneself, while becoming leans towards the whole of life – the ongoingness of life itself.

Hope as Process

Hope as process is all about spirit... Spirit entering into existence, spirit being manifested. Spirit entering, spirit manifesting only occurs along the path of intent. Spirit enters existence through essence – the pattern of intent. It is through our living from and enabling of essence that spirit is manifested. Spirit brings ongoing and uplifting vitality to our life. Joy is a common experience of life in the spirit.

What brings hope, what works for all children, are processes organized around essence... processes that enable the seeing of essence, the bringing forth of essence, the living from essence. Such processes enable our beingness to be nourished by, enriched by, to be manifestations of spirit. When processes are devoid of essence – organized around existence, for example – beingness becomes disconnected from spirit... beingness looks to material – to energies of existence – for a sense of aliveness... a process that unfolds in the direction of increasingly coarse energies, in the direction of a life increasingly devoid of spirit. A spiritless life is a hopeless path… a path whereupon we become more and more externally defined; less and less intrinsically expressed.

As we become more serious about entering into the waters of life in and from the Spirit – Spirit entering through essence into the working of the world – we quite naturally innerly experience a sense of risk… a clear sense of risk that becomes more real as our seriousness increases… seriousness as a process increases as we more vividly see the necessity and do-ability of what we are ever more strongly being drawn towards… that which we are developing the courage and confidence to say "Yes" to... a yes that emerges from the truth of our instrumentality… of our not being the source, but rather like all of life, an instrument.

It is quite common for us to enter into our consideration of becoming an instrument through the perspective of existence… seeing risk in terms of our current culture, its expectations and its way of working. And as we image our stepping outside of the culture, we can, with doubtless clarity, feel and know – innerly experience – the likely wrath of current culture. A not unexpected cultural reaction given the way of working of culture: culture works to sustain intended patterns, to resist that which intends, is seen as, is working at shifting that which the current culture is organized around.

We can, however, begin our contemplation from the perspective of essence. Here we shift from ourselves to what really is at risk… and, as our understanding of intent, intended ways of working deepen; as the path of intent becomes more visible, more vivid; we begin to see life much more wholistically… we consider what truly works for all children, we better see the ultimacy of our current path; and gain a deeper sense of the hope in the unfolding path of intent... all of which adds meaning and significance to our "Yes"... and ultimately, wholistically we can return to self... seeing self in the light of the whole, in terms of work and role, our called work... work that requires community; the fulfilling of our intended instrumentality. And now risk itself shifts in meaning and understanding, an aspect of which is brought to the fore by the story of Rabbi Zhuka – the wisdom he imparted at the time of his death:

Rabbi Zhuka was an elderly and highly revered person in his community. As he lay near death, Rabbi Zhuka was asked, "Given your years of study and contemplation, what do you think the kingdom of God will be like?" To which he answered, "I don't know." Then after a bit of a pause, he said, "What I do know is that as I approach the kingdom of God I won't be asked, 'Why are you not Abraham? Why are you not Isaiah? Why are you not Moses?' – rather, I will be asked, 'Why are you not Zhuka?'"

Each has a purpose, a role...
a personal calling, a personal mission...
work to do, a potential to fulfill...
all are equal, each is significant.

Love as Process

Love as process is all about will... the will that makes all things possible... the will force that is behind the whole of creation, that which sustains the ongoing upward unfolding – the unfolding image of the Source...

It is through our becoming instruments for love entering – for love to enter into the working of the world – that Thy will can be done, on this earth at this time.

Christ, as one of his going forward gifts, gave us the princi-

45

pal of *loving one another as I have loved you* (JN13:34) The essence of the love of Christ, his acting as an instrument of the one who sent him, is his making it possible for us to realize our potential – to do, as he did – by fulfilling the intent of the Source. His surrendering to the will of the Father, accepting his instrumentality, is a manifestation of his *love for God* (MK12:30) – the other of our going forward principles – a showing of the way for us as well.

Love as will, entering through essence – the pattern of intent – is free of the entanglements of existence… the entanglements so familiar to us – our expecting a return, the expectation and need for gratitude, etc.

Thus, as we surrender to being and becoming instruments for love entering, we enter into a process of shedding – the shedding of entanglements… a shedding which moves us towards an inner sense of calm and peace… an inner sense that does not take us out of the realities of existence, its drama and dynamics, but rather gives to us a centering capacity – an ableness to be more true, regardless… and through this, as we begin to get a deeper, more meaningful experience of the truth of love, we move closer to the essence of truth itself, and its intended way of working…

…And the truth shall set you free (JN8:32).

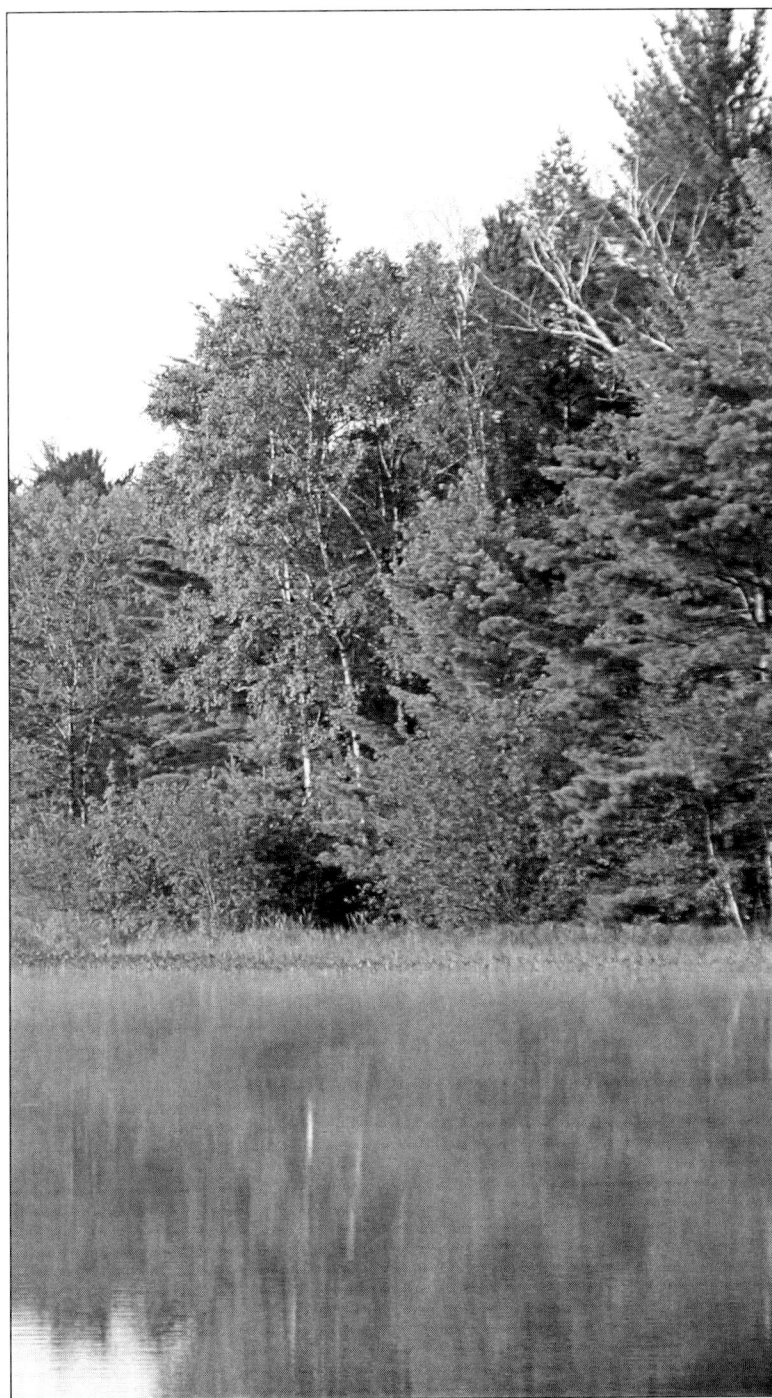

If all-inclusive love is not present in the process,

all-inclusive love will not be present in the outcomes.

There occurs from time to time, the necessity to bring about the revitalization of that which has been brought into being... a revitalizing process that, like life itself, is a forward moving, upward evolving process. Now is such a time for our country... a time for an upward shift organized around our instrumentality, our purpose; and the truth of our not being the source... a process sustained and nourished by the ongoing development and unfolding of intentional ethics... ethics reflecting a life of the whole perspective, and seeking understanding with regard to right and good... right for humanity, good for the whole of life... an orientation required for pursuing that which works for all children in the world.

Volume Two…

INTENTIONALLY REVITALIZING OUR COUNTRY

Developing Serious Intent with regard to the Work before Us

An Emerging Process for
Developing Serious Intent Regarding
the Work Before Us

What follows is a collection of letters and papers, writings that have emerged through reflections following some serious dialoguing with a number of people regarding subjects of interest... subjects of significance, not only to themselves, but to our country, and beyond. These reflections emerged in the face of the need for developing an essential thought base for a wholistic country strategy, the need which is becoming increasingly evident and obvious to a growing number of Americans, and as well, to people across the world, people who look to us for leadership, virtuous leadership, ethical leadership, the nature of leadership that leads to seeing hope. As such, this collection is more of the nature of a diary or journal of unfolding images, than what one normally thinks of as a book with chapters. As the thoughts develop, they build for us a charcoal sketch of sorts: a wholistic image of the preparation called for begins to come into view, a clarity that will continue as more and more of us see the work before us, believe it must be done, and wish to access the will necessary for taking up our part – our work and roles – in that doing.

The papers emerged through reflection and dialogue. Reflecting and dialoguing are complementary processes aimed at seeing wholeness and gaining understanding of intended ways of working... processes not lacking in spirit and energy, but processes aimed at seeing... the nature of seeing that nourishes and develops serious intent.

The hope in the sharing of these letters and reflective papers, is that they provide some starting points for further reflecting and reflective dialoguing, enabling the developing of serious intent regarding the real work of now, the work of...

Revitalizing our country in a way that...

> *moves us towards wholeness, away from that*
> *which divides...*
>
> *works for all children – all children of the world*
> *– now and into the future...*
>
> *brings the world of our making into congruence*
> *with the world of intent...*

such that the intended unfolding of now – the particular
advance in humanness along the path of our becoming
fully and truly human – can, through a conscious "Yes,"
emerge and be realized.

Terry P. Anderson
September, 2011

America's "Yes"

Our ship, our country's ship, the ship the worlds' people look to – for better or worse – is floundering upon increasingly rougher seas, stormy seas of our own making... and we, the people, flail about in ways that exacerbate the aimlessness, the rudderless see-sawing course of our ship. There is present a great temptation to seek "safe" harbor, to put down an anchor of 'how it used to be,' and how we cannot shift, cannot move to a higher plane... how we, lacking in necessary character and resolve, are doomed... thinking and behavior totally incongruent with the character of the people and process by which this country came into existence.

This is not a time to set an anchor, rather a time to set sail... to plot a course of intent, to set our compass towards right and good – right for humanity, good for the whole of life. It is not a time to extract the last bits of sustenance from that which has been put in place; but rather a time to realize our potential... as a country, as a people of earth... a time to intentionally pursue becoming fully and truly human – fulfilling the intent of the Creator. It is a time for taking up the work of bringing the world of our making into congruence with the world of intent... a time for America and her people to say "Yes"... to take up our intended role, our intended work.

The Urgency of Now

Reflecting on "Now is the time of potential" being a necessary boundary for us to willfully cross, the old phrase, "Time is of the essence," came to mind. A common meaning of that phrase is the notion of quick action: the patient is very ill – the doctor must operate; the baby is on the way – must get to the hospital; the river is rising – must evacuate while we can; etc. It seems that the question relates to understanding the reality of the situation and the risk involved. No doubt we are at a critical juncture as a people of earth, a time of advancing humanness or regressing. It is also a time of little trust – little trust in political processes, in the integrity of institutions, etc. – and a time of little faith. We have asked, what do we, what should we have faith in? For those that hold that "Seeing is believing," there is much evidence casually and readily available. Yet with all this, we are left without the common tool of reason – without a convincing argument based on irrefutable logic. For this time of now requires the changing of heart and mind – opening hearts and developing minds, the minds needed for the work. We have said that we write from intuition, to intuition. Thus it seems that it is intuition that needs to wake up to the urgency of now.

The intuition of wholeness is much more effective and efficient than reasoning... once she sees the picture, the truth of it all, she has all she needs to go forth... no proof needed. So what is at work at this time: more and more of us are experiencing the need to move towards wholeness. Moving towards wholeness is not about taking a negative stand towards divisiveness, but rather lifting up the hope in potential, seeing the hopelessness of the path we are on, and stepping onto the path of intent, always remembering that it is not a path one can travel alone; it requires community. The need to make a real shift is intuitively obvious. The urgency – the need to go forth now, while the patient is still breathing – is innerly growing stronger by the day. The urgency of now, when fully embraced, commonly calls out "What do we do?" Which brings us to the reality of…

Ultimately, the perspective you hold –
where you start your thinking from –
determines the path you take, the direction you move in –
what you move towards, what you move away from.

To change hearts, to open hearts to wisdom, starts with changing the starting point of our thinking. Perhaps the most critical first step in this shift is to accept there is no savior, no one person that we can put in a position of power and who can then act in a saving way, saving us from what we know in our hearts is the likely outcome of our current ways. In regards to earth, the savior role was filled long ago, it is still occupied; no vacancy there. America is a people-led country; the people develop the thought, and the processing of the thought creates the void into which leaders can move. The reality, at this time, is thought starting from a problem perspective has no resolving power… so forget that. Which brings us back to faith: In what do we put our faith? Do we put faith in the intent of the Source? Do we put faith in our smartness and cleverness? Which path is the most familiar… which is yet untried… which does intuition see the most hope in… which brings real meaning and significance to the here and unfolding now… which does not cause us to separate our way of working/doing business from our hereafter professions of faith… which takes us towards bringing the world of our making into congruence with the world of intent? Critical questions with intuitively obvious answers… questions and answers that create sufficiently whole images that – given today's reality, the truth of the situation – naturally create a sense of urgency within… the urgency of NOW.

Contemplating Life...
Some Realities of Here and Now Living

Reflecting on life, our life and living, that which we experience from the time of entry to the time of exit, we notice some foregone realities... some of which were true then, are true now, and will continue to be so.

Some of these realities, those that lean towards the physical, are more visible – more readily observable – than others. Take for instance the force of gravity... an active force that influences and impacts all. We see it at work as we watch a young child learning to walk... struggling to stay upright... planning each attempt, each step – striving to go further, to extend each effort beyond the previous, likely not conscious of the notions of gravity, but fully aware of its presence, subject to its realness none the less... a realness that we, towards the end of the visible segment of life, become reacquainted with, a renewal of our awareness, as the possibility of falling returns.

Then there are those realities that are equally present, equally as consequential as the force of gravity; but less overtly visible... more seeable through reflection than direct observation... more brought forth in the context of meaning, purpose and significance... a deeper sense of real – what is really real. One such reality, the common law of earthly life, is that *ultimately, the perspective you hold, where you start your thinking from, determines the direction you move in, what you move towards, what you move away from.* A reality that exists not only for the one, but is equally true for a community, a country, a people; and like gravity, it does not require conscious understanding on our part to be actively present... to be at work in our everyday life... influencing our path, our pursuits, that which we hold as significant, as insignificant – that which we pay attention to, that which we ignore.

58

With further imaging of life, we notice we are first and foremost living creatures of life... sharing with other creatures of life many of the same realities... realities brought to mind through seeing at work such notions as breathing, eating, drinking, growing, developing, becoming... out from which a oneness of Source and nature, along with wholeness and systemic working, become apparent; which in turn provides a basis for the seeing of systemic roles – those unique roles and work common to life's members, roles responsible for sustaining the interconnectedness that is present throughout all of life, roles that are not always fully understood, honored, or enabled... but ones that are actively present and uniquely critical within and to life.

A readily observable example is present in the pollinating work of bees... the work that is taking place as a bee moves from flower to flower... the work that represents the essential purpose and role of the bee... work that not only provides sustenance for the bees, but also serves to sustain life – the life of the whole, all of life. Pollination, a particular form of fertilization, is the process by which fruit and other foods come into existence. In addition, pollination is critical to the ongoing cycle of life, a cyclical process we can begin to image by seeing the forming of the fruit, the forming of the seed within, the sowing of the seed, the sprouting of the seed, the growing of the plant... so critical is pollination to life, that if pollination ceased, so too would life on earth as we have come to know it. Einstein once pondered this subject. His pondering began with the thought of there suddenly being no bees on earth. His thoughts followed a path of no bees, no pollinating; no pollinating, no food; no food, no people. And as to how long it would take before we ceased to exist on this earth, he recognized that it would be a very short time, perhaps as short as four years. Finally as we reflect on systemic relatedness and roles, we notice some diminishment in some common notions of hierarchy... particularly those related to positional place and status.

Seeing and gaining some understanding of the wholeness and systemic working of life naturally brings to the mind some questioning regarding role – the systemic role of humankind… questioning that moves us towards the beginning and the intent of the Source… earth was not created for man; rather man, we humans, were created for earth… created intentionally, not accidentally, as members in the larger community of life. We humans, like all creatures of life, have our own particular uniqueness – uniqueness of role and work – uniqueness that using the word, "human," seeks to capture – to indicate and bring about a differentiation between ourselves and our fellow creatures of life… a differentiation necessary to our developing understanding of our purpose, role and work on earth. Perhaps unique to humans, when it comes to understanding, is our access to both the manifested works of creation and the revealed word. Both of which reflect the expressed will, the intent, of the Source. Both of which through reflection and dialogue can deepen our understanding of our work and role on earth – in particular with regards to the here and unfolding now.

It is interesting, as we reflect on our way of working in regards to gaining understanding of truths, to notice it is not uncommon to first gain some insight as to what something is not… a certainty of what something is not often precedes an imaging of what it is. For example, take the word, "dominion," a familiar word in regards to man's role on earth. Given its origin one might, in an automatic sort of way, have an impression of "to lord over" – implying a particular sort of responsibility. What quickly follows, however, is some "is not" clarity. Surely dominion does not reflect an intent for us to diminish, disenable, or destroy that which has been created… nor would we expect such behavior with regard to intended ways of working of life on earth.

60

Nor for that matter, would it be reasonable to expect – given that we are intentionally created as members of life, existing within life, not separate from the whole of life – that our role, our work and purpose on earth, would not reflect life's realities.

Reflecting further along the path of the word brings to mind some clarity brought to us by a great teacher, some two thousand or so years ago... clarity expressed and captured in his response to his followers regarding prayer... a response to their request for a teaching relative to prayer and praying... a prayer not so much for himself, but for them after his departure. Some clarity regarding our role emerges from an excerpt of this somewhat familiar prayer: *Thy kingdom come, thy will be done, on earth as it is in heaven* (MT6:10). From this it seems quite clear that our role is not so much about imposing our will upon the earth, but more about working and living in ways congruent with Thy will... ways of working, of going about our business, requiring conscious attention to intended ways of working... ways essential to the ongoingness of life, life in the here and unfolding now... ways worthy of serious intent on our part.

This same teacher would introduce a new perspective, a new starting point, for our continued advancement in humanness... advancing our ableness to take up and fulfill our intended unfolding role... role and work that move us in the direction of becoming fully and truly human – a realizable potential, a true possibility. Enfolded within this starting point was the essence of the Source, the essence of the revealed word, and the essence of the teaching. From this systemic essence emerged two commandments, both of which were anchored in love – *Love the Source; Love one another* (MK12:30; JN13:34)... two commandments to serve as guiding principles, going forward principles, principles relevant to and necessary for our progression in the here and unfolding now... principles brought to life – made real –

through the new truth of inclusivity, a truth that transcended the limitations of blood – of lineage and heritage... a new starting point which did not, however, disconnect us from the realities of life. We were to continue as living human beings, but with the new possibilities, new potential... possibilities and potential yet to be realized... a realization that requires the taking up of the work that is now possible, the work that is now being called for... work that does not require the imposition of our will upon this earth; rather work that brings about congruence with willful intent – with intended ways of working... work that reflects the intended coming of the kingdom... work that, given the realities of this time, our time, this time of now, requires the taking on of a life of the whole perspective... a life of the whole perspective, a systemic approach... a perspective and approach that makes possible our moving towards wholeness and away from that which divides... and our doing so in ways that work for all children, all children in the world... bringing the world of our making into congruence with the world of intent.

It is through philosophy, the wisdom and discipline of philosophy, that the life of the whole perspective and approach can become real – practice-able, actively present, and at work within life on earth. Not just any philosophy, but rather a philosophy that is whole enough, complete enough, to truly deal with current realities and with the work at hand – the real work before us – and perhaps most particularly, it must be whole enough, complete enough, real enough, to transcend the rigid, disenabling, limitations of existing ideologies... those collections of ideals that by their very nature – their segmented, narrow slice nature – lack true resolving power... the power necessary for upward reconciliation – an upward shift along the path of our intended becoming... a transcendence that itself would make possible the sharing of ideals that more truly reflect intended humanness – more essential ways of being human... of being human with regards to ourselves, with regard to the whole of life... ideals, not the least of which, are those related to work – meaningful work, called work, our work on this earth. And finally, our philosophical discipline must lend itself to the realization of our potential – our potential to be and become fully and truly human: our potential to fulfill our role – to carry out our earthly purpose and work.

A seemingly useful closing thought to this writing: reality, real reality, is invisible to the common eye of reason. It is through the eye of the heart that the real, the really real becomes visible... that an unfolding seeing begins, that an awakening – a dawning of understanding – emerges within... a dawning that brings forth a seeing light, a light sourced in wisdom – the wisdom of intent... an inclusive light, a welcoming light to the authentic, intentionally working eye of reason... a light through which reason can blossom, flourish, and take up its intended work... truly seek to fulfill its potential, its potential to bring forth into existence that which is congruent with intent.

Developing Serious Intent

Developing serious intent is the critical element – certainly the initial work – of this time of potential, a work that requires accessing of wisdom of intent. From the perspective of potential, serious intent is the means for entering the path of becoming, the way of moving towards wholeness, away from that which divides… the way of our becoming fully and truly human… a way that surely is congruent with *the way and the truth and the life* (JN14:6), and necessary for the living out of the commandments to *Love God* (MK12:30) and to *Love one another as I have loved you* (JN13:34).

Behind serious intent is the requirement to acknowledge a Source, an intentional Source beyond ourselves. Serious intent is the process whereby our essence – pattern of intent – becomes awake and operative in regards to work that we are drawn towards… work that is along the path of our calling, our purpose, our reason for being here. Serious intent is to be thought of in a way similar to wisdom – not as something we have or seek to get, but rather a process. With wisdom, the process is "accessing wisdom"… with serious intent, the process is "developing serious intent." Serious intent is present – at work within – when our intent is in harmony with the intended working of the world, of life on earth… with the whole of life.

The Work Before Us;
The Work Within Us

These thoughts seek to bring some imagery and understanding of the work within us, and the work before us – the urgent work of now... images and understanding that can be further enriched – more see-able – through reflection and dialogue.

Work is a common subject and a central organizing phenomenon with regards to our taking the path of intent...

the path of realizing our potential to become fully and truly human... to fulfill the intent of the Source.

It is not uncommon for work, the taking up of particular work, to require some focused work within – some inner processing and organizing – to bring about that which we need to understand, that which we need to be; so that we can authentically engage the work before us... the now work of this time of potential: the work of bringing the world of our making into congruence with the world of intent, with intended ways of working. The central theme of this work is the necessity for moving towards wholeness, and away from that which divides... all the while conscientiously working to ensure that the pathways and pursuits we choose will indeed work for all children, all children in the world, now and into the future. Congruence with intent, wholeness, and working for all children in the world are the systemic parameters of the work before us.

The work within calls upon the intuition of wholeness. It seeks to bring voice to intuition, courage to conscience... develops ableness in regards to wholeness – the seeing of things wholistically, seeing the whole, developing imagery of intended ways of working within the whole... a conscious seeing and awareness of wholeness such that we have a firm basis for conscience to operate against, conscience not so much in terms of right and wrong, but more so in terms of right and good… and in particular, what will work for all children in the world, an ultimate expression of conscience at this time of potential.

Inner processing and organizing also lends itself to the necessary work of awakening us to the truths of what is inherently within; the essence of who we are as living human beings: the truth of our intended instrumentality… the uniqueness of each and all, with the recognition of the commonness of our instrumentality – as a person, as a community, as a people of earth. Whereas it is the inner work, the work within, that gives clarity to *who we are*; it is the outer work, the work before us, that brings clarity to *why we are* – our work, the work of our heart, the work of humanity, our "pollinating" work, our role in regards to the ongoingness of life.

Turning towards the outer work – the taking up of the work before us – our thoughts return to the notion of realizing potential and a truth thereof: in the absence of taking up the work before us, there is no realizing of potential, no manifesting of spirit, no advancing of humanness, no fulfilling of the intent of the Source, no possibility of the necessary upward shift in the way we live and work. It is useful to remember that the work within, and the taking up of the work before us, are in reality a systemic cycle – a cyclical process where each develops the other; each requires the ongoing reciprocal nourishment of the other. Thus we can see that the stirring that more and more of us are experiencing has a twofold purpose: that of turning us innerly towards the work within – the particular work of now; and that of turning us outerly towards arenas of work we are drawn to – arenas of work within the whole of the work before us: the bringing of the world of our making into congruence with the world of intent.

Reflecting on the process of engaging the work before us, and on the common experience of hesitation and reluctance to "cross a boundary," has brought forth some thoughts. Reflecting on current reality and current ways of doing things, reason would argue it is necessary to create a logical, irrefutable, scientifically validated argument… an argument that is overwhelmingly convincing, and truly undeniable. Anything short of that will not bring about the intended shift. Wisdom would offer a very different notion… wisdom, who is present to intent and understands intended ways of working. She understands that the work before us is the work of the heart… work that calls for the creation of an intentional presence… the taking on of a stance that reflects a willful conviction, one that is organized around intentional truths… an entering into and engaging arenas of work, acting from heartfelt conviction and persistence – a truth and conviction that is readily experience-able by others… all of which contribute to an ongoing intentional presence… a stance and presence that may quite naturally feel a bit hazardous, but a necessary stance for us as a people to transcend the intuitively obvious hazard before us, the hazard before the whole of life.

Finally, as a sense of closure entered, I was treated to images of the voice of intuition speaking from the courage of conscience… bringing about the intended unfolding – not from us, but rather through us… Spirit entering through intended instrumentality.

Wholistic Approaches

Wholistic approaches require the seeing of the whole, its intended ways of working... its essential processes and related systems. This type of approach anchors itself, uses as a starting point, the perspective of potential... versus a perspective of problem, of problem solving. This approach, for example, would see waste as a potential to be realized, versus a problem to be solved. Wholistic thought calls upon and works through intuition – the intuition of wholeness – and is deepened and enriched through reflection and dialogue. As the imagery of wholeness begins to develop and emerge, realistic and practice-able ways and means of implementation become visible – unfold before us... a seeing of what to do, and ways of "can do" become more and more substantive, more clear and concrete. Along with this increasing clarity comes a sufficiently whole understanding such that ethics and ethical principles can be articulated. Thus the most effective of our tools – the ableness to be ethical, to live above the law (the law being the means for establishing the minimum/lower boundaries for regulating ourselves) – can once again be present and alive in our managing processes.

For example, wholistic approaches offer real and practice-able ways for authentically moving towards and achieving energy security... and for doing this in ways that put in place sustainable wealth generating processes. Truly sustainable wealth generating processes have a twofold systemically interwoven nature. As such they not only enable us to effectively deal with the economic realities of our life and living in ways that bring about the creative possibility of a better life for our children – all children in the world – they also, simultaneously, work to maintain the vitality and viability of the life generating processes of earth – of life itself.

An example of a wholistic approach is the wholistic regeneration of plastics – plastics made from oil. Beginning our thoughts with oil, we notice a few things. Oil, which we extract from earth, has taken mother earth forever to make. It is this notion of forever that earns oil the designation of being a non-renewable, limited resource. There lies within a barrel of oil, however, the potential to produce structures – like plastics – that themselves can last forever… to be in reality, perpetual products… or perpetual waste. We are quite familiar with the burden of perpetual waste – the impact on landfills, ecosystems, economics, etc. We are, perhaps, less familiar with the notion of perpetual products. Wholistic regeneration of plastics (for example, nylon carpet, plastic bottles, and so on) makes real the potential for perpetual products. Wholistic regeneration – the returning of the plastic products to their essential building blocks – allows not only the regeneration of the original product, but also the possibility of even higher value products. Thus what was (is) considered waste can become part of an endless cycle of perpetual products… all of which can occur and continue to occur without the need for obtaining new barrels of oil. Plastics that have already been produced are in fact "barrels of oil" in inventory… perpetually available. This fact, of having barrels of oil in inventory, allows for a significant reduction in demand for new barrels of oil. It is this significant reduction in need that directly contributes to our energy security. And the fact that wholistic regeneration is readily doable, says the reduction can be achieved within a short time. Thus a rapid advancement in energy security is present before us, not only in terms of diminishing outside threats to ourselves as a people, as a country; but also in terms of reducing the deleterious effects on life, the whole of life on earth.

The common experience of wholistic approaches is the seeing and uncovering of the unexpected… unexpected possibilities and benefits; and even the "hoped for" expected seems to become more real, more able to actually happen.

For example, in regards to energy security, the benefits of disentangling the securing of oil from the philosophical approach and thinking behind our foreign policy shows up. Further, the ability to retreat from or avoid altogether the getting of oil from arenas of hazard to ourselves as a people and/or those critical to life – for example, estuaries – is anequally real benefit. Perhaps, more close to the unexpected is the seeing that the innovation demand for wholistic regeneration of plastics is that of systemic integration versus technology invention. Being free from the necessity for new technology invention allows for rapid implementation, and thus a real reduction in the need for new barrels of oil within a short time. Other seeing lifts up favorable economics, rightness and goodness with regard to the life processes of earth, truly sustainable wealth generating processes, etc.

As we leave the example of wholistic regeneration of plastics, it may be useful to contrast this approach with the common experience of recycling plastic. Quite common within the recycling of plastic is the creation of a downward cascade of lower and lower value products… which ultimately lead to waste – waste for the landfill, waste to be burned as fuel. Imaging the process of hand-me-down clothing, where clothing ultimately ends up as rags – rags that get thrown away – is a helpful example.

Prior to closing this writing, a beginning point for another wholistic approach is offered: that of automobiling… "automobiling" versus "automobile" because it allows us to see beyond the structure (automobile) to see the whole… to better see what is really at work… and to see the potential value realization that lies within automobiling. We see, for example, the opportunity for rapid and significant reduction in necessity for new barrels of oil by a man-on-the-moon-like determination for "oil free automobiling"… and the obvious value of that to energy security. Within this wholistic approach we see the simultaneous possibility for greatly reducing the current burden of health care costs by "injury free automobiling." Also coming to the wholistic mind's eye are possibilities for eliminating other troublesome interferences with automobiling, such things as gridlock, etc.

Further reflection on automobiling lifts up systemic integration of existing technologies as key to rapid advancement along this path. But even more significant than that – in an initiating,leadership way – is serious intent; serious intent having the character and requirement of open declaration and inner conviction... the nature of conviction made possible through love entering the process. Serious intent opens us up to creative energy... provides organizing and coalescing power to its use... as well as a crisp focus for investment – committed investment, the investment of effort, material, energy, finances, enabling laws, etc., required to ensure the sustainability of this path.

Perhaps the most obvious seeing that comes about through perpetual products and oil free automobiling is the huge number of barrels of oil that no longer are needed and thereby how secure our energy security can become. But other, equally significant benefits appear as well. We also see the inherent limitation of incremental approaches such as recycling of plastics, increased m.p.g. standards, etc. Clearly seeing the limitations of such incremental approaches allows us to shift significant levels of our attention and investment towards more beneficial and permanent solutions – solutions that in themselves bring about evolutionary step changes. Also, the number and variety of businesses that naturally emerge and are spawned from these value realizing processes is quite incredible... businesses that are manifestations of the truth that within each and all lies potential... potential to be realized. Along with this plethora of businesses comes clear and meaningful directional guidance to educational and developmental processes regarding work – meaningful work… spirit manifesting work… spirit lifting work.

Finally, useful to remember throughout this work:

> *When it comes to waste, there is no away…*
> *but there certainly is potential to be realized.*
>
> *Hope, real hope, lies with intent, with our being intentional… in our being and becoming in harmony with intended ways of working.*

Where Do We Start?

The notion of sides – are you on this side or that side, be it green, red, blue, etc. – is a predominant happening in our country. If we pause a bit and reflect on our current world – the world of our making – it is obvious that none of the common sides, the arguments for the perspective they hold, is whole enough to deal with what is before us – especially in terms of that which works for all children. We can begin to see that it is not so much which side we are on, but rather *where we come from*. For me, I choose not to come from a particular side, but rather to come from potential. Coming from potential – from intent – is whole enough, complete enough to enable us, in a serious way, to take up the work of bringing the world of our making into congruence with the world of intent... and to do so in ways that work for all children, all children in the world.

Which brings me to the comment made by my brother-in-law recently, a comment which I experienced as an authentic from-the-heart expression of truth: "We have to change the whole world." Apparently my brother also experienced the intent and authenticity of this expression; because he responded in a serious way, "Where do you start?" And after a bit of a pause, he offered, "Do it here; start in Ishpeming." Beginning with ourselves, within our community, is the most real, the most hopeful, perhaps the only true approach. The current reality – the world of our making – requires the development of wholeness of thought within community... out from which leaders will emerge... the nature of leadership and leaders called for. This truly is an issue, a piece of work, that starts with the people, within our communities. It is not one whereby a solution, a true path, will come from outside; not from the current ways of working of the various established entities of our country.

Where do we start? We start from spirit and potential, from seeking congruence with intent... we start with that which is required such that we bring into the world that which is essence-based virtue sourced value adding.

73

Awakening the Spirit and Potential of the Upper Peninsula

The Upper Peninsula (the U. P.) of Michigan is the place of my birth, a rugged land of minerals, timber, Great Lakes shores and cold snowy winters… a land I love for its capacity to build character while it awakens you to the beauty and demands of nature. I was called upon to reflect on this land from a repotentializing perspective – with the hope of creating a charcoal sketch of the potential of the U.P. that provides a basis for further development.

If efforts we undertake are to be repotentializing in nature – as opposed to improving what is – we must begin our thinking from the perspective of potential versus the perspective of problem. In regards to the repotentialization of the Upper Peninsula, we would begin by anchoring to and indexing from the virtue of the land itself. Potential is always realized by working out from or being sourced in the essence or core virtue of that which we are trying to realize the potential of. And so we would first have to get a working image – supported by a verbal expression – of the essence or core virtue of the U. P. Now there is an expression (trademarked, I believe) that, to me at least, would be a good starting point – a place from which to begin reflection and dialogue – that statement (from my memory) being, "The Upper Peninsula: Rugged as its coastline, tough as its winters, independent as its people." …remembering, of course, that virtue/essence is more of the nature of truth – in that we are not seeking an absolute, but rather a working statement that through time will unfold and deepen in meaning.

Working from the virtue of the land, we could develop a living philosophy – a "Yooper" way of living and working – out from which would emerge, develop and evolve value adding processes – value adding processes that would not only reflect the essential character of the U.P., but would also provide the organizing point for doing business and for businesses. Doing this would certainly make possible – move us closer towards making real – a business teacher's statement to his students, "You don't have to leave the U. P. to be successful in business," a statement that I perceive as not only a belief, but a dream – a dream of the character and nature expressed by Dr. Martin Luther King Jr., which is important to remember because for those who would take on a leadership role – the role of leading from virtue – there will be the requirement to draw forth spirit and energy accessible only through true dream and vision.

Continuing, here are some thoughts on essential value adding processes:

> Tourism. From the perspective of harmonizing with the virtue of the land, tourism would develop, not as the "entertaining type," but as the skill, and self-reliance development made available through the energy field of the U. P.

> Metals/Metallurgy. Regardless of the ornateness of the artifact or product, it would have "inbuilt" the toughness and capacity to sustain its performance – ongoingly – without complaint. None of the metals – be they castle hinges and doors, or space age material – would easily or readily give way to fatigue.

> Woods/woodworking. It is a strength and an essential requirement for maintaining the spirit of "Yoopers" to see the beauty in all... regardless of the tough or challenging work that may follow. Witness how often you hear or

find yourself saying, "Isn't that beautiful," in regards to a snowfall… knowing full well it may take a day or more to "dig out." As I have reflected on "Yooper" value adding processes, the image of the natural (essence) beauty of the wood, regardless of the ruggedness of the work for which it was designed, would always be visible and present.

Education. Regardless of subject matter, education would have a character building component – a component that acknowledges "independence" which perhaps transcends itself to "manifesting uniqueness," but in either case never loses sight of "we're in this together" (for example, in a snowstorm), and thus the necessity for working together, helping each other… a component that develops the capacity for "plain speaking" – for straight forward interaction.

A few thoughts about schooling, and the development of our children and resources form the last piece of the charcoal sketch. I recall an experience I had when consulting with a company that produced turbines for jet engines, and the interaction with an accomplished metal sculptor who I met through some community development work. What I discovered was the technological understanding required to produce the castings for large sculptures was of similar depth to that required for casting jet engine turbines. The point here is that the nature of value adding processes will require an evolving depth of craftsmanship – of the nature and tradition of craftsmen who develop and advance the technology of their work. The institutions that would be called upon to play a role in these processes would need to advance metal and wood technology beyond that which is currently understood. Tourism and education would require similar advances in understanding and process delivery.

Well, that is the charcoal sketch. There is no question that the sketch covers a bit of territory – hopefully enough territory to build an image of sufficient wholeness that we gain a "taste" of its do-ability. As I looked over the sketch, I experienced a real sense of hope and possibility – hope because the virtue of the U. P. is still accessible (it has not been artificially obscured), and hope from the knowledge that there is still present sufficient "U. P. character" that could be awakened and out from which could emerge leaders and leadership... people who would respond to and lead from virtue, those who would see it, and experience it as a true calling.

Criticality of Intentional Ethics

Earth was created for life to have a place to enter into the universe.

It is through water that life emerges, is nourished and sustained.

It is through water that each member of life, all members of life, the life of the whole and the whole of life on this earth emerges, is nourished and sustained.

All water is living water... and all life is intended to be open to and receptive to nourishing waters.

Therefore all water is holy water... sacred water... water being the essence of the process of life itself.

Water is the means by which the Creator carries out intended work in the world.

It is intentionally unethical to diminish the life-givingness of water, disenabling the intended role of water in regards to life.

This reflection on water is a taste, a drink, of the criticality of intentional ethics... intentional ethics being those that lead us to congruence with intent and intended ways of working.

Some Thoughts About Thinking

Where you start your thinking from determines the path you take. For example, if you start from economics, you cannot get to value. If it is value that you seek, you need to start from virtue... virtue then brings you to intent; which in turn requires philosophy – a disciplined approach – to live out and bring about intent, to realize value. And if your thinking is to take into consideration our current realities – the world of our making – then by necessity we start from, come from potential. Coming from potential allows wisdom – the wisdom of intent – to guide reason, in particular our reasoning. Wisdom guiding reason is critical to our thinking, given the truth that if we, as a people, are left to our own – our own reasoning unguided by wisdom – our situation is, without a doubt, hopeless... a potentially discouraging reality. There is hope, however, real hope that lies within the truth that through love all things are possible... love being perhaps the ultimate virtue... which brings us back to intent, the intent of the Source... which brings us back to the starting point of these thoughts...

Urgency for Starting
Our Thinking from Intent

There is no doubt in my mind that hope, real hope for all life on earth, lies in bringing the world of our making into congruence with the world of intent. Which brings us back to where we start our thinking from. Starting our thinking from intent brings an understanding of our being an instrument, not the source – an essential instrument, but clearly not the source. Accepting our instrumentality – detaching from the illusion of our being the source – is urgently needed. Immediately following is the understanding that there are no real solutions possible from our smartness (reason unguided by wisdom; science acting as source, etc.). Love enters through instrumentality. *Through love all things are possible* (MT9:26; 1JN4:8)... remembering that love emanates from the Source of creation. The most urgent and real thing that can be done is to come to grips with and surrender to this truth: *one Source; all else instruments.*

Science is grounded in cause and effect. It uses fractionation as its process. Both enable the accessing of knowledge, sometimes quite rapidly, but very slowly does understanding emerge, especially understanding related to wholes and systemic interaction. Now if science started its thinking with seeking to understand intended ways of working, looked at things wholistically and systemically, accepted the guidance of wisdom and its instrumentality, it could play its intended role. Anything short of that, we will/life will be at the mercy of incremental approaches that we intuitively know are in reality hopeless. So if we are "betting the farm," more hope and realness are to be found in love, than in the current ways of science.

The Good in Hopeless

Recent interactions on critical ecological issues have, through reflection, engendered some thoughts on hopeless – our being void of hope… thoughts on an authentic experience of hopeless – of our seeing no hope, particularly in regards to our understanding and our sense of certainty relative to now – to what is, to what is now unfolding. I find it interesting, in these type reflections, how often wisdom that has been shared or lifted up to us comes into our mind and it is not uncommon for both the wisdom we access through the intuition of wholeness and the wisdom we gain through experience to enter into our process. From my experience, I have found that when I honor the wisdom, it serves to both deepen and enrich the reflection in ways that enable my moving more innerly towards essential truths and away from the outer – the often disturbing dynamics of the external.

"There is good in all." I often, as was true during this reflection, hear my grandmother's voice expressing that thought, that wisdom. What then is the good in hopeless became an organizing and energizing question for my reflection, a question not seeking a reasoned answer, but rather seeking to see hopeless at work. What follows is some of the seeing.

Hopeless is often a pre-condition for having real hope. The seeing of our situation as being, without doubt, hopeless makes visible and often makes possible our acceptance of an ultimate truth: the truth of our being an instrument, of our not being the source. The realization of our being powerless, of our lack of ableness to change the reality before us, can, and often does, cause us to look to a higher source – to turn away from ourselves and towards a source greater than ourselves… and to surrender to that source, surrender our will – our ego – to Thy will. That is the potential good, the virtue in being hopeless… its true gift.

Looking back on experience and history, we can see this at work. An example that comes to mind is the conviction and understanding of a professional psychiatrist working in a home for drug and alcohol addicted women with children, women who commonly were pregnant at the time of entering the home. She once explained to us that even with all her training and expertise; nothing really worked until the woman acknowledged and surrendered to a higher power. Once that occurred, with wisdom guiding reason, hope and a forward path could begin to unfold.

Further reflecting took me back to experiencing Christ as he surrendered his will to the will of the Father… a process that was for him, imbued with the certainty of hopelessness… human hopelessness with regard to what was about to unfold – the cup that was before him, the surrendering of "self as source," the authentic acceptance of instrumentality. Similarly, by our so doing, we are truly putting ourselves "on the hook," a level of commitment very different from that which self-as-source can realize. Some other seeing emerged regarding Christ's expression of *I am the way* (JN14.6), some imagery that can enable our moving towards essential truth and away from dogmatic pursuit. At essence, the way of Christ, the way of following Christ through the narrow gate, is through the surrendering of self as source, through embracing self as an instrument… an instrument for taking up and carrying out intended work.

Lastly was imagery regarding the beatitudes (MT5:3-12). Here we can see hopeless – our being void of hope – as a precondition for authentically engaging and entering the pathway of the beatitudes (the opening beatitude being *Bessed are the poor in spirit…*). The surrendering of "self as source" (including our self as being the source of love, good and truth), and embracing self as instrument is a prerequisite. There is much beauty and joy here that lies within this pattern and process. For it is through our being hopeless that we open ourselves to a path, a way, of hope… hope made possible through our instrumentality acting in accord with the intent of the Source… the very Source of all, the very Source of the love through which all things are possible. Thus our being hopeless – void of hope – can lead to a path and a way of hope… providing of course that we have faith, true faith, in the intent of the Source.

After reading this reflection I noticed a fair emphasis on self – self as the starting point, surrendering self, self as instrument, etc. I also understand that at this time of potential, community (not so much self) is the smallest whole. What then will community taking up the way look like? Perhaps a seeing yet to come; perhaps one that I will not be privileged to see. But I have confidence and take heart from an understanding of the process of upward unfolding. Here the essential truths of the previous are enfolded into the unfolding; emerging with added depth and wholeness. And of course, the gathering, with serious intent, of two or more can generate the seed from which community can unfold… a regenerative seed.

Sorting Out... Seeing the Now Need for Intuition of Wholeness

Ongoing interactions have evoked some imagery and thoughts... thoughts and imagery that seem to follow the pattern of "sorting out"... a common experience as we work to develop serious intent. We notice as we reflect on our own life history, that sorting out is a process that shows up from time to time. Each occasion being somewhat unique and requiring its own similar pattern and need as we reflect on human history... a pattern and need that comes to the fore as more and more of us experience the unfolding intent of this time... of what is upon us now.

Now is the time of potential... a time of moving towards wholeness, away from that which divides... a time for taking up the soul building work of bringing the world of our making into congruence with the world of intent... a time for building the soul of humanity... a time that requires the calling upon and utilization of the intuition of wholeness – that which is required to gain access to the wisdom of intent, the wisdom required to guide reason.

Embracing, entering into, participating in, enabling this intended unfolding brings to the fore some anchors and truths... truths that have been present since the beginning:

> *There is a Source (we are not the source) of the whole of creation, a Source, a will force behind the whole of all... an intentional force out from which emanates intended ways of working.*

> *Earth was created to be a place for life to enter into the working of the creation. Earth was not created for man. Man was created for earth.*

> *As living human beings, we, like all of life, are intended instruments; with real roles, real work to carry out.*

An aspect of sorting is differentiating the real from the unreal; and at this time of potential, differentiating that which is whole, that which is moving towards wholeness, from that which is a fragment, a segment, that which serves and seeks to divide; all of which is ultimately dependent upon and determined by where we start our thinking from. We can experience the working of the start point of our thinking by reflecting upon processes common to religion and science, both of which deal with the notion of mystery and efforts to become more knowledgeable – through reasoned interpretation – in that regard. They look to theological theories – theology – and scientific theories as ways of organizing thought, organized thought being both necessary and useful to the gaining of knowledge and insight... to bringing this knowing into daily life and work. For example, the scientific theory of evolution contributes greatly to the study and experimentation that leads to the advances in life, biology and medicine that we enjoy and benefit from today.

Reflecting further we notice a tendency to restrict or self-limit the domain, the "territory" of study. It is common in science to focus on the material, the structural, the physical, the energies (including some life energies) aspects of our existence. And not uncommonly, holding the principle that only that which is, or can be reduced to, material fact is real. Reality, in a sense, is reduced to the provable. Turning now to religion, I am reminded that my reflections are somewhat limited in that my experience is mostly in regard to that commonly thought of as Christian religion. From readings and interactions with others it seems likely that some of these thoughts will carry over to other religions as well, particularly in regard to the use of theological theories and reasoned interpretation to generate dogma, advance knowledge and practice. With that in mind, we can look at the common domain, the self-limiting arena of religious thought, some of which kind of naturally, perhaps

85

not intentionally, comes about through habitual patterns. For example, the pattern of anthropomorphism has the effect of reducing the mystery to that which is explainable in human terms, in human characteristics.

Other limitations come about through conclusions/convictions as to what is an acceptable/authentic source against which reasoned interpretation can be applied – often relating to a particular organized thought base/reference. Another limitation shows up in regards to who or what has the capacity/authority to engage in the reasoned interpretation of the thought base… a limitation shared by science. One other limitation, one critical at this time of potential, a time of upward movement along the path of our becoming fully and truly human, is the choosing of salvation – being saved – as the central forming core of Christian religion… a reality that often obscures the expression of will, the intended way of living as we went forward, given to us by Christ in the form of two commandments… commands commonly expressed as *Love God,* and *Love one another as I have loved you* (MK12:30; JN13:34)… expressions critical to upward movement in the here and now.

Well, perhaps that is sufficient exploration in regards to the notion and process of sorting out. What I notice in that reflection is the lack of wholeness reasoned interpretation brings about – in part by the self-limiting domain, but also by its fractionating way of working. I also notice a tendency to look at what is needed now in terms of what we have experienced and come to know through reasoned interpretation… a tendency that causes us to elementize, reduce to segments, that which is intended to be whole – be it a thought or a living system. We cannot move towards wholeness, or gain wholistic understanding, through reductionist thought processes. Shifting the starting point of our thinking is now being demanded of us. In looking at science, we can see both the magnitude and potential in shifting our aim and way of working from gaining manipulative knowledge and expertise, to seeking understanding intended ways of working and becoming expert in harmonizing with intent… shifting from creating a world based on our wishes, our desires, to pursuing congruence with intent. With a bit of reflection on common current practices in food production, eco-system interaction, medical procedures, etc., we can see manipulative knowledge at work.

So then, what is both real and necessary at this time of potential is our turning towards the intuition of wholeness, the seeing and accessing of wisdom… to consciously utilize that which does not have the established position of reasoned interpretation; nor the familiarity and comfort enjoyed by the pattern of reason and logic. It is obvious that lifting up and pursuing that which is a bit contrary to established practice will take conscientious effort and courage. Wisdom guiding reason is certainly a new starting point that carries a bit of irony with it. It is ironic that the potential and value of reason will be realized through the process of wisdom guiding reason.

Seeing What is at Work Behind Our Doing

Before beginning this reflection, it may be helpful to image an example of the working of structure and structuring with which we are all familiar. Consider eating. Structures are entering our bodies, structures such as food, beverages, etc. We can envision the nature of structuring of our bodies themselves that takes place as a result of the structure of the food itself as well as our habits of eating – the ways of eating. A common saying speaks to our intuitive understanding of the working of structures and structuring: "We are what we eat."

The more I have contemplated structure and structuring (outer and inner), the more I have come to realize the significance of seeing the structuring at work behind our doing, significance in regards to developing the understanding and leadership processes required to bring about the step change of now. From a process perspective, structure and structuring are at the essence of the understanding out from which leadership can emerge. Here are some thoughts that have emerged as I have contemplated this subject. These thoughts are examples of what can be seen by holding structure/structuring in mind… a seeing of what is at work, and a seeing that may make visible what needs to be at work.

Looking at significant country issues reflectively, we see some things. Pursuits seem to be anchored in "what is," and improvement of "what is." Pursuits are sourced in, directed by the ideology of the pursuers. It would be of value at this point to take time for a couple of reminders about ideology, ideology being a set of ideas, aims and goals. Ideologies serve to both guide and encompass (create boundaries for) action. They often have the effect of creating closed system thinking, that is, you are either "in" or "out," and by their very nature, they lack sufficient wholeness and capacities to deal in real ways with today's reality.

88

Let us return to current ways/working, that of being drawn to and energized by an issue – a "what is" issue. The issue is seen as a "problem to solve." We then tap into current culture ideologies to get an image of an ideal (for example, the idea of helping inner city kids to one day live in the suburbs "to be like us," to be able "to live like us," etc.). We pursue a problem solving approach and expect some status and recognition regarding goodness – being seen as a good person, a source of goodness, etc.

To further our thoughts relative to the working of structure and structuring, we turn to theology. Theology without living philosophy collapses to ideology... an ideology with a character of rightness (perhaps self-righteousness) that allows and justifies actions – taking action that a more wholistic perspective (common sense wisdom) would see as unethical and/or immoral – neither right nor good.

We began this reflection with "From a process perspective, structure and structuring are at the essence of understanding out from which leadership can emerge." It is important to see what is at work, the structuring behind our doing – to become conscious of it versus automatically/culturally following it, perhaps because that is "how we do things." Now if an essential aspect of our work, bringing the world of our making into congruence with the world of intent, is to become part of our inner structuring (versus ideological obedience), we then look to the living philosophy of potential, reflective dialoguing, wisdom seeking, etc., to generate the images of intended working which become the understanding that is foundational to leadership processes at this time of upward shifts.

And so we see the usefulness, the essentialness, of an envisioning capacity, a working understanding of structure/structuring, for those called, those saying "Yes" to this work of now, the work of bringing the world of our making into congruence with the world of intent.

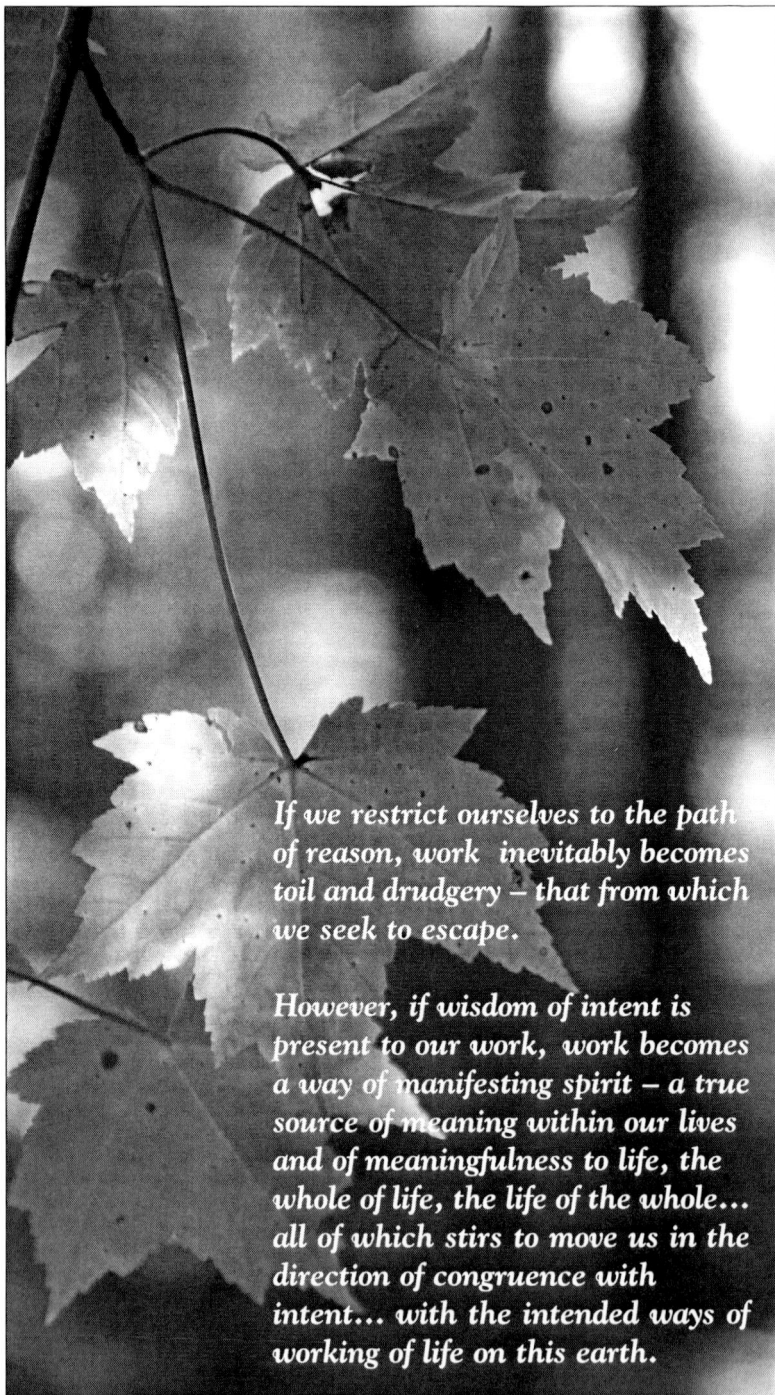

If we restrict ourselves to the path of reason, work inevitably becomes toil and drudgery – that from which we seek to escape.

However, if wisdom of intent is present to our work, work becomes a way of manifesting spirit – a true source of meaning within our lives and of meaningfulness to life, the whole of life, the life of the whole... all of which stirs to move us in the direction of congruence with intent... with the intended ways of working of life on this earth.

Vision Coming From Potential,
And Leading From Potential

Some recent interactions have generated thoughts on vision... vision coming from potential, and leading from potential...

Vision is a wholistic image borne out of a philosophy that would allow us to live a life we believe in. Vision, in turn, brings life to our philosophy through a systemic seeing – seeing the working relatedness of what needs to come together. Vision inspirits us and is an ongoing source of spirit and willfulness as we strive to bring about – bring into being – that which we envision... a spirit and willfulness that enables our being, and being experienced as, authentic. It is the active presence of vision – our connectedness, keeping it alive within – that serves to develop and strengthen our commitment to the work required. As vision dissipates, so too does will – leaving us only motives and motivation as a means to sustain effort. Motives and motivation can energize us, but do not have sufficient will power to realize intended potential.

The carrying out, the bringing into being, of a vision requires consciousness of, and conscious attention to, our philosophical approach, that is, coming from the living philosophy of potential versus a philosophy of problem. Also, necessary to be present in mind and heart, is clarity in regards to essential virtue – what we have thought of as our "guiding star" for our pursuits... essential virtue having the character of advancing our humanness, of bringing us more into congruence with intent and intended ways of working. We can see this in the autism work, with its essential virtue of "inclusivity"; and in the intentional community entrepreneuring work, with their essential virtue of "harmony with earth." Essential virtue serves as both the entrance to and the aim of our path... a kind of alpha and omega.

With this seeing of path, we then look to our working philosophy – that which reflects the uniqueness of our approach, and that which needs to be embedded into the process of bringing together the systemic elements required to realize the potential of the vision. Our working philosophy provides a systemic image – a seeing of that which we need to be disciplined about. It brings to life and makes real, a disciplined approach that acknowledges and effectively deals with current reality in a way that enables the upward shift – the necessary advancements in humanness and congruence with intent, intended ways of working. It is through the working philosophy that wisdom enters – is present and active… a practice-able wisdom… the wisdom required to guide reason as we go forth... a wisdom that can be actively present in our way of working, a way of working lifted up and guided by and through principles… principles such as our being grounded in "intentional ethics" in intentional community entrepreneuring, and likewise being grounded in "evidence-based practice" in the autism work. If we reflect on this, from top to bottom so to speak, we notice how that which comes before colors and guides that which follows; while that which follows brings into practice – to the "shop floor" – a manifestation of vision… a true expression of our living out the vision; of our fulfilling intent.

Coloration and guidance enables the maintaining of integrity from vision to reality. It works to ensure that the strategies we pursue are indeed congruent with intent, with the essence of the vision and the philosophy… congruent strategies, versus strategies emerging from habitual patterns or how things are currently/commonly being done "out there." Consciousness of these common practices is important, but equally important is our not being captured by them, nor should they become a source of direction – a useful instrument, perhaps but not a source of direction. Lastly we have, as tools for maintaining integrity of intent, audit

92

and evaluate. We can, through periodic reflection and dialogue, ask ourselves questions like: did we carry out our actions as we intended; how true a reflection of intent were they? And in regards to evaluate, questions such as: what value did we realize; can we see movement towards advancing our humanness and towards increased congruence with intent and intended ways of working?

And finally, vision is central to leadership and leading… both in terms of those who take up the leadership role required by the vision; and in terms of being conscious of what, at any given time, is leading our thinking. Pausing for reflective questioning of what is leading our thinking is critical to our staying on path. For example: is self-centered extraction or reciprocal nourishment leading our thinking? Other examples could be created around economics and rights versus right and good.

In leading from potential, enabling the seeing of potential and the experiencing of what is possible is the nature of the leadership process. A particular aim of this leadership process is the enablement of conscious choice by those who would join the work, conscious choice being necessary for a sustainable commitment to the work involved, conscious choice being very different from that which is achieved through arguing, convincing, proving, etc.

Be Alert to Wobbly Hedgehog Syndrome…

We need to be alert to "wobbly hedgehog syndrome" which appears in living human beings (singularly and collectively) as a logic disorder that causes us to wander off the path of intent. Some common symptoms are: starting our thinking from economics versus starting from essential virtue/value and generating economics/reciprocal nourishment around that; honoring current ways of doing things versus intended ways of working; reason turning a blind eye to wisdom –

particularly the wisdom of intent; grounding our actions in legality/rights versus the right and good of intentional ethics; high frequency of "out-running our headlights," that is, reason charging ahead with insufficient understanding, doing it "because we can," etc., etc.

Country Energy Strategy...
An Example of Seeing Potential through a Wholistic Approach

A recent note regarding an energy supply issue stirred thoughts about energy strategy – the necessity for and absence of – in regards to our country. In my musings I came across some information on thorium, thorium in place of uranium for producing nuclear energy. By reflecting on this example of replacing uranium with thorium, we begin to see the potential in a wholistic approach, an approach that demands of us a different nature of commitment and pursuit than is currently active in our energy strategy... an approach that has the potential to work for all children in the world. Some intriguing aspects of thorium are...

> Oak Ridge Laboratory developed a process for thorium in the sixties. More development is needed, but feasibility has been established. Its biggest weakness was that the thorium process does not produce plutonium which is needed for nuclear weapons.

> Thorium reactors could produce electricity at a cost comparable to burning coal... and with no greenhouse gasses.

> Thorium reactors are far safer, cheaper, and easier to operate than uranium fueled reactors. Thorium reactors do not melt down and they produce less waste, with the waste being much less radioactive than that from uranium fueled reactors.

> Thorium is more abundant and easier to mine and process into reactor fuel. The United States has the largest supply of economically available thorium rich ore of any country in the world.

Current nuclear waste could be used as fuel in thori um reactors... essentially eliminating currently existing and accumulating hazards.

Thorium-fueled reactor design has advanced such that it can come close to a perpetual process – that is, the process generates waste which becomes fuel, a cycle that may need very little new fuel.

There is more energy contained in thorium reserves than in all fossil fuels on earth.

This all sounds quite promising in the sense of what becomes possible when we think more wholistically. We have been slow to pursue this change since we have urani um, but nuclear waste is a significant and growing problem. This might cause us to wake up. Coming from potential versus problem could cause us to put focused effort on perfecting the thorium process we invented fifty years ago. Others seem to understand this. China, India, Israel, Norway, and Russia, to name a few, are actively pursuing this technology. They see distinct and obvious advantages to their country in such pursuits.

Transcending fossil fuels (requiring us to see stored carbon as a source of perpetual products versus as fuel) is a path of high hope for our country, for all people, for all of life on earth, which requires us to question the current starting point for our thinking. Coming from a country energy strategy versus from economic extraction may be a good place to start. It takes little imagination to see the economic and wellbeing potential in a country strategy that includes thorium technology.

It is interesting and somewhat reassuring to see that the ultimate direction for industry, regardless of product, is that of coming from and aiming towards the virtue of being perpetual – perpetual products and perpetual processes in regard to energy. I can see the notions of "sustainable" moving up to the more wholistic virtue of "perpetual." I have always thought it is important to differentiate that which is truly evolutionary from that which maybe common, popular, etc. For a long time, business has been moving towards commodity – commodity versus uniqueness of offering. Driven in a large part from the mind of efficiency and self-centered extraction, commodity is definitely not an evolutionary value; it is more aimed at milking that which has been produced. In recent discussions regarding intentional entrepreneuring in community, we dealt with the working of space. As you move towards commodity, space decays, leading to less and less space to operate in, and to more aggression being required to gain sufficient returns to stay alive. On the other hand, as you move towards uniqueness, space becomes infinite, able to nourish all who operate in accord with that.

Segmental Economics/Wholistic Economics

Further discussion on country strategy has lifted up some thoughts on economics – a popular orientation and starting point for much thinking. Remembering the reality of life, *the perspective you hold – where you start your thinking from – determines the path you take and the direction you move in*, may be helpful as you continue through this note. The conversations lifted up two, distinctly different, orientations regarding economics, one being segmental economics and the other being wholistic economics.

Looking at segmental economics, we notice some common characteristics of this orientation. The tendency here is to focus on a segment, often a segment separated out from some larger whole, and not uncommonly, organized around a singular point – for example, point of sale, point of use – and/or a particular individual or self-interest. When reducing itself to cost, segmental economics tends to generate a fractional representation of total cost, a representation often expressed in finite terms – for example, dollars per kilowatt hour.

Contemplating wholistic economics, some images of process and character emerge. There is a seeking to understand the working of the whole and particular systemic relatedness – a tendency to go beyond the singular to include community/country… whole of life. When considering cost, wholistic economics works to get an understanding of total cost and benefits beyond the singular. Looking at our previous thoughts about thorium as a source for nuclear energy provides a useful starting place example. Reflecting on the potential of thorium nuclear energy in the context of uranium/plutonium nuclear energy, we can begin to image some more wholistic approaches and some particular systemic notions. For example, we can see a nuclear arms/disarmament treaty evolving into a cooperative effort between countries of the world to develop a viable thorium process, eliminating the need for uranium/plutonium processes. And by so doing, freeing the potential for peaceful uses that lie in nuclear energy. Thus allowing states viewed as rogue states to have plutonium-free nuclear energy for power – a commonly stated intent for their nuclear energy program. And if we look at the energy needs of the poor and developing countries (as well as the energy thirsty developed countries) we see much potential and economic benefit as well – not the least of which is the potential and possibility to raise the quality of life and standard of living across the planet. Further imaging of all the issues of the uranium/plutonium/nuclear waste process enables the seeing of the total and true cost of the uranium, etc., process, and, I would expect, the gaining of some clarity as to the potential value and cost (reduction?) of the thorium process. As this imagery of potential unfolds and develops, I notice within myself an inner experience of uplifting spirit and a growing sense of hope… which I am seeing as an essential aspect of the virtue of wholistic economics. And in addition, I am more clearly seeing the resolving power, the power of wholistic economics to enable true resolution to the significant issues of our time… a resolution not possible through partial approaches.

Mere Mere's Wisdom

When I was a young person I often heard my grandmother – whom we called Mere Mere – say, "Don't throw the baby out with the bath water." As one who grew up with taking a bath in a small tub of water which was picked up and carried outside to be emptied, often used to water plants, I could not imagine someone actually throwing the baby out with the bath water. Later on, I did get some images that added credence to her statement. A recent thought expressed to me brought vivid imagery and renewed credibility to Mere Mere's wisdom. As we reflected on the downsizing, budgeting, cost cutting turmoil in our governing systems, processes and structures, a path forward was suggested, a process that could take place around our kitchen tables, at the local pub, etc. Most simply what she said was this:

> Take a piece of paper. Draw a circle in the middle of the paper. In the circle write down the intended purpose, the essential reason(s) for the entity's exis tence, its intended way of working. For example, our government was intended to be of the people, for the people, by the people; power was to flow from the people to the governing structure. With some clarity within the circle add capacities, processes, systems and structures necessary to carry out the essential intent – essential intent being the "baby in the bath water"… a process that allows for meaningful shedding of the unintended, the non-essential.

I could see in this timely suggestion, a deeper sense of the wisdom of Mere Mere's statement… and the necessity of our going back to intentional purpose, essence of work and working, if we were to avoid having our personal preference, the removal of that which we do not value, do not like, etc., as being the source of our decisions. The essential work – the work of developing the thought base from which those who would lead could lead – always falls to "we the people." And so we should not be surprised that this work is work we in our communities are called to do. And, in the doing of this, we would certainly have more clarity from which to answer the critical question, "What is leading our thinking?" and equally, if not more important, the question, "What should be leading our thinking?"

It was exciting to see through this initial suggestion, the relevance of Mere Mere's wisdom in the context of today's struggle. The ongoingness of the wisdom is heartening as reflected by a comment by another person, "I am not sure that in the way we are going about things, we even recognize there is a baby in the bath water"… a comment applicable to many processes beyond the governing process… seems like a good place to end this note.

Essential Virtue/American Spirit

Some further interaction around wholistic strategy for revitalizing our country has brought forth some additional images and thought… images and thought that help move previous reflections towards wholeness – a more wholistic image in regards to a strategy for our country…a natural occurrence in that it is wholeness that we seek when we come from potential. So then, is not a strategy that would lift up the world, create a better world for ourselves, all of humanity, and the whole of life – that nature of strategy made visible through our imaging of the potential and possibilities of thorium as a peace enabling source of nuclear energy for the world – a truer expression of the essence, the intentional purpose, spirit and role of America? …an authentic manifestation of the *compassion of equality?* – compassion of equality being the forming core, the essential virtue actively present in the forming of our country, and, as our history shows, ongoingly accessible. *Compassion of equality* being the very virtue which, when we are acting from and through, creates within us a real sense of wellbeing, an inner experience of "This is who we are" – who we really are, who we are intended to be… an inner sense of rightness and goodness… a manifestation of the spirit of America, a spirit not so much emanating from us, but rather flowing through us, a spirit made possible through the acknowledgement of a Source of creation, and the truth of our instrumentality… of our having an intentional role.

The processing of strategy brought forth some additional imaging and understanding of the working of space, in particular decaying space and infinite space. We began to see how natural it was in times of decaying space to turn towards problem solving approaches… to react to the issue of decay in ways that intensify and energize the problem solving approaches of reason… a process that generates disturbance and tension within and between the other systemic elements of space – that which we commonly experience as my space, your space, our space – and also bringing with it the not uncommon associated energies of aggression and conflict, all of which tend to aggravate and deepen the realities and experience of decaying space.

Coming from potential – with wisdom guiding reason – allows us to move towards and into infinite space, infinite space being the nature of space required for realizing potential – for manifesting uniqueness, for realizing the potential of each and all, for realizing the potential of one's country – ours and others as well. The space that enables both the advancing of our humanness – moving towards becoming fully and truly human – and our wisely dealing with an inherently natural aspect of ourselves: the desire to move up planes of existence, to have a better life for ourselves, and for future generations.

Now obviously moving towards infinite space requires a shift in our approach, in the starting point of our thinking... and a shift in our pursuits, and that which organizes our pursuits. Useful and necessary to any intentional shift is firm grounding and guidance.

There is, emerging from the work on intentional entrepreneuring and intentional community, some understanding that can provide some useful grounding and guidance. The anchor point of both of these efforts is a working philosophy imaged as the systemic triad of virtue, ethics and potential. Emerging from this working philosophy is a systemic set of guiding principles:

> Add no infrastructural burden.
> Effectively utilize community resources.
> Seek processes and pursuits that engender
> reciprocal nourishment.

And further, is an unfolding and developing understanding

related to particular business endeavors, particular communities, particular called work of individuals/communities, etc... all of which require deliberate attention to virtue, ethics and potential.

A *final thought...* We know from experience that a spirit manifested is available forever to all. From the wisdom of Mere Mere and her daughter, Helen, comes this caution: *No matter what path you take, it cannot be a path that diminishes humanness; one that reduces who we are as a people... one that reduces who we are intended to be and become.*

Starting Our Thinking
From the Compassion of Equality

Remembering that *ultimately, where we start our thinking from determines the path we take and the direction we move in, what we move towards and what we move away from*, brings these thoughts:

If we start our thinking from the perspective of problem, seeing homeless for example, as a problem to solve, we move towards thingness and away from beingness; we tend to focus on what things need to be put in place to resolve/fix the problem... a focus on thingness that begins to engulf the person as well. This is true even in the presence of thinking/approaching the issue in a positive (versus negative) manner. As thingness gains strength and beingness diminishes, so too does the possibility for the presence of love in the process diminish. A sense of doing good may be active, but this too brings with it the hazard of our moving towards the illusion of our being the source, and away from the truth of our being an intended instrument.

If we start our thinking from the *compassion of equality*, holding the intent of "seeing beyond what is" and embracing the truth of our equality (versus one up / one down, for example), we move towards beingness, towards being and becoming more truly human... a beingness that allows love to enter the process, the love through which all things are possible. Now wisdom can guide reason, and that which is brought into existence can reflect that which advances our humanness and moves us, as a community, towards wholeness and away from that which divides. Which brings us back to familiar territory: the time of potential.

Now is the time of potential, a time for moving towards wholeness, away from that which divides. Wholeness calls upon willful beingness; thingness, by nature, moves towards that which divides. A unique aspect of this time of potential is the reality that community is the smallest whole; the being shift called for requires community versus the more familiar notion of an individual, one person, etc. Another reality of this time of potential is that left to our own – thinking of ourselves as the source – is a hopeless path and process. Surrendering to our instrumentality, moving away from our illusion of our being the source, is the path of hope… hope in that love can enter the process, and through love (remembering that we are not the source of love), all things are possible. Thus we can see that to come from potential, versus problem, at this time of potential requires that we start our thinking from the *compassion of equality*.

There is a parable related to the wisdom of and the necessity for putting new wine in new wine skins. The new wine is the *compassion of equality* and the new wine skin will reflect the truth of our intended instrumentality – be free of illusions concerning source. It will reflect community as the smallest whole – versus the self, and other essential characteristics as well. And so, issues like homelessness provide both the opportunity and potential for us, as a community, to move towards wholeness and away from that which divides… opportunity for our community to come from and access the *compassion of equality*… to move towards becoming fully and truly human… as intended. An opportunity that through intentional working enables our community being and becoming *at home* – and through wholeness becoming *at one* with the Source… the Source of each and all, the Source of the whole of life.

The Hazard of Entering into Thinking
at the Level of Concept

It is a common experience of life to be energized by a concept – a particular ideal that we find very attractive... often seeing goodness and not infrequently a sense of rightness as well... and it is not uncommon to actively express this concept to others in exciting and energizing ways with the aim of getting them to join in this pursuit. I only have to reflect on my teenage years to get a taste of this process.

This process does not disappear with aging – the aging of a person, the aging of a country. It is as active today as it ever was. The necessity for wisdom guiding reason is understood to be a critical point of focus at this time. Some reflecting on the working of thinking may help us see things more completely, more clearly in regards to enabling conscious choice and wise decisions.

Entering into thinking at the level of concept is a very natural thing to do... concept brings with it a nature of seeing that often brings joyful excitement – a seeing of what would be possible, an image of that which is inherently attractive to us. Often accompanying this is active pursuit and planning – increasingly detailed planning unfolds. However, if our aim is wise choices and pursuits, it behooves us to pause to consider what needs to be in place – what capacities, what ableness is demanded; as well as bringing to light the philosophy (not to be confused with ideology – a collection of ideals) behind the concept, and the ethical principles required to intentionally guide and manage the living out of the concept, philosophy and principles that not only serve to enable discipline and guidance, but that which also takes into consideration our current reality – our current ways of doing things.

There is today a plethora of concepts, a literal cacophony of voices calling out to us. There is also a growing recognition of the active presence of greed and the absence of ethics in a number of our essential processes... greed and ethical absence organized by a lack of wholeness – a self-centeredness..., greed and ethical absence leaving few, if any, of our institutions and organizations untouched... a realness and reality requiring serious consideration as we seek to engage particular concepts through thinking more completely. As interesting and attractive concepts emerge, we may find it of value to consider the experiential wisdom present in "Don't throw the baby out with the bath water" – let us not discard the organizing purpose and intent. As we reflect on this and other concepts in the light of current reality and in terms of what needs to be in place, philosophy and principles brought to the fore some cautionary wisdom of the past:

> *There is no superman.*
> *Don't turn the fox loose in the hen house.*
> *There is no escape.*
> *It's not what it looks like.*
> *There are no partial solutions.*

Further imagery brought to mind a saying from a fellow I worked with back at the lab. Jim was a person with a habitual pattern of misadventure. He would sum it up by saying, "Well, it seemed like a good idea at the time..."

Wisdom Guidling Technology

I struggle with the notion of today's technology being "more than amazing." I have tended to look at it as a tool which, when used intentionally, can contribute to the advancing of our humanness. I have some uncertainty about the current explosion of mechanical/electrical devises – regardless of how fast they move and organize electrons/particles of light – in terms of enabling upward advancement of our humanness... a better world for each and all, including the whole of life. As far as the internet's role in the current Middle East's upheaval – the move towards democracy – perhaps one day it will be considered in the same light as "Poor Richard's Almanac," the back room pub conversations, etc., which occurred during the mid to late 1700's. Much will depend on the wholeness and completeness of thought that was behind this rapid exchange of information... its lasting power, and the willfulness of the people. Let us hope that willfulness and wholeness of thought are present – actively developing and strengthening – and last but certainly not least, that reason understands the necessity for it to be guided by wisdom, the wisdom of intent... a requirement if this effort is to move along the path of intent – a path of upward movement in humanness. It is probably just me, but when the word "amazing" comes into play, my mind lifts up images like planting a tomato seed and eventually being able to eat a home-grown tomato... and as one of our own said in song, "The only two things that money can't buy are true love and home-grown tomatoes"... taken together, they remind us that *if love is not present in the process, love will not be present in the outcomes.*

The Process of Sorting Out

I recently heard from a recipient of many of my writings, most recently some of these wholistic country strategy papers. The following is my response to the note.

It was good to hear that you are still actively seeking and seemingly engaged in a process of sorting out... a fairly common process for more and more folks... perhaps influenced some by the richness of uncertainty going on around us as well as a sense of realness to that which is being bantered about as having some affect on our pattern of life. Then again, there is a growing certainty that *now is the time of potential – a time for moving towards wholeness, away from that which divides, and doing so in ways that work for all children in the world.* In a real sort of way, the stage is set – everything is in its place, there are roles/work to be fulfilled and taken up. The question of how to join in the process, a process that we feel drawn towards, but one that requires an active yes, no invite, just joining in, on our part, is commonly being asked... a yes carried through work, a wholistic perspective of work (versus my job, what I am currently being paid for, etc.).

Sorting out does call upon reflective inner processing and reflective dialogue/interaction with others. The Path of Potential writings are a useful source for both (there is a host of such writings on our website). I am reminded of the life of the honeybee. You might recall that it is common for some bees to live about 21 days, the first 18 of which are spent in the hive; the last days outside the hive pollinating (the essential purpose of bees). A truly beautiful thing about their process is the way they communicate the location of the flower to the others. A single bee, the finder of the flowers, can find his way back to the hive, but does not have the mental capacity to direct the others to the flowers. Thus the dance – a mind creating dance – whereby the

110

image – magnitude, direction, etc. – is created in a way that the bees can return to the flower patch, do their essential work, and bring back nourishment to the hive. To me at least, I see in the process of the bees the working of a reality of our time, that being: *community – two or more – is the smallest whole*.

Another aspect of joining in seems to be the having of some anchor points – conscious references – that we carry with us. I notice that some have found value in the truth – *one Source, all else instruments*. Other conscious references have emerged through the taking up of the work, anchor points that have relevance to a broader scope than that through which they emerged. For example, the working philosophy of virtue, ethics and potential emerged through work on business regeneration, the ethical principles of add no infra-structural burden, effective utilization of community resources, and reciprocal nourishment first emerged through work on autism. These principles are also actively present in the work on intentional entrepreneuring in community, as well as in efforts with young people, aimed at helping them experience life and make life real, work that lifts above the artificial life provided through media. There seems to be both the personally significant and that which reflects the community nature of this work at this time.

Finally, the two notions of *one Source; all else instruments* and *now is the time of potential* seem to act as boundaries, necessary boundaries, for us to willfully cross... that which we have to innerly process and accept as truth and reality. Nothing much gets manifested until this comes about... often with some hesitation, some natural clumsiness, but with little or no fuzziness. Given that, we can then go forth coming from potential – bringing that perspective into our daily working and living – stepping out onto the stage... a "coming out" of sorts.

Well, that is a bit of what was evoked in me through reflecting on your note. I enjoyed your comment about "expecting no final exam." I guess that is really true… especially since a final exam carries with it the sense of completion – a false sense in regards to the ongoing unfolding evolutionary process. I am reminded, however, of the story of the Rabbi Zhuka and the final question he was certain would be asked: "Why were you not Zhuka???"

The Time Is Now

A firm basis for conscience to operate against;
an ultimate expression of conscience at this time of potential
is...

> *What will work for all children, all children in the world.*

~ ~ ~ ~ ~ ~

Ongoing interactions have stimulated reflections on work for all children, on pursuing that which works for all children in the world, have brought to the fore some thoughts regarding schooling, educating, intentional writing and critical thinking.

"Don't let your schooling get in the way of your education" is an old familiar adage... an adage that serves to remind us of the contrast between knowing and the processes of experiencing, seeing and understanding. Further contemplation brought forth some imagery of schooling, not only as an element of one's education, but also looking at it from the perspective of community; thus these community organized thoughts regarding the essential work of schooling – looking at schooling in the context of the larger whole it is intended to serve, looking at what is schooling from a particular perspective, the perspective of community... community being the larger whole which schooling is intended to serve:

The essential work of schooling/educating the children is to develop ableness within to bring run-up resolutions and solutions to the emerging issues and problems of today.

> *Run-up ways advance humanness and enhance (versus deteriorate) essential life processes of earth.* Run-up ways represent a significant shift in pattern from what is becoming an almost total focus on arresting run-down... a segmented problem solving approach.

113

Run-up pursuits are wholistic and systemic in nature. They demand an orientation towards and a pursuit of an understanding of intended ways of working – within an arena of work, within a field of endeavor, within a community, within life processes of earth… an understanding that provides a basis for ethics, intentional ethics… for our living and work-ing in intentional – ethical – ways. Reflecting upon the wholistic and systemic character of run-up work brings to light some images and understandings of the realities of today…

Real shifts, necessary shifts of today, require communi ty: Community is the smallest whole through which the needed shifts can and will emerge.

Several other aspects of reality show up as premises – the truth of which becomes more visible, more concrete, as we reflect and dialogue on our experience, on what is occurring today.

There is no escape. First off, as we came to under-stand with regard to garbage, waste, effluents, etc., there is no away.   Similarly, there is no escape – no island of refuge, no insular pathway for ourselves or the children, including no escape from the global issues of today… issues of hunger, divisiveness, ecol-ogy, for example. And…

There is no fence. There is no fence, no fence to sit upon, no place from which to passively observe, to await an externally imposed resolution – one that works for all children. And…

There is no superman. There is no superman, no earthly savior – man or woman – who will be elect-ed by the people and magically make things upside right. This understanding is perhaps the most hopeful of all because it diminishes the illusions of wishful thinking and brings reality and focus to the work before us… the reality that it is in and through community that upward resolution will emerge – including those who will lead, lead from wholistic images, and systemic thinking.

Underneath these premises is the truth of our accountability as living human beings, members in the larger community of life. That is:

> *We are responsible for the structures we bring into existence, and are accountable for them as long as they are present on earth…* an accountability and responsibility that calls upon us to bring the world of our making into congruence with the world of intent. Yes, what lies before us, and around us, is a world of our making; the upward forward path is a path of con gruence with intent. We are responsible for the structures we bring into existence… for all structures from laws to houses… from those used to produce a product to those "left over" after we are finished using the product… from the structure itself to the structuring the product and its related processes produce.

Looking back at particular times in human history, we notice particular thoughts and processes emerge that are critical to our evolution – to an upward shift in humanness, true movement along the path of our becoming fully and truly human. This time, our time, this time of potential… this time of now, is such a time. Thus the emergence of writing – intentional writing – whose aim and work is to lead our thinking such that we can willfully take up the work before us… writing that both reflects critical thinking and engenders critical thinking… critical thinking regarding that which we need to think critically about.

In this regard, we see that intentional writing and critical thinking are systemically related… they are a complementary – each completes the other – pair… they are members of a system that includes listening, reflecting, reading, dialoguing, etc…. a system that takes direction from the essential work, the critical work of today, the run-up, negentropic work before us – the work of advancing humanness, enhancing essential life processes of earth… the work that represents a real pattern shift from the almost exclusive focus on arresting run-down of today.

Looking further at intentional writing and critical thinking in the context of today; in regards to their way of working, some other realities and essential/intended ways of working come to the fore… images and understandings that add depth and direction to the work before us.

With regard to intentional writing, a reasonable starting point is the way of working of pen to paper. Taking pen to paper is a mind organizing process; whereas taking fingers to a keyboard is a thought organizing process. Now building a particular mind is a common requirement of work. We see this at work in various schoolings, for example, building an engineering mind, a mind for business, the mind of a musician, etc. Given that the work of today requires approaches that are wholistic and systemic, the mind organizing capacity of writing by putting pen to paper will be an important developmental process for the worker, enabling the development of a form of writing – and thus interacting – perhaps not so commonly used today… but one that is nevertheless critical now.

It is worth remembering, and paying attention to, that even as writing evolves, the functional skill common to all writing will be necessary and called upon. And too, the life enriching character of the narrative impulses we gain from novels, poetry, etc., are neither diminished nor dismissed... but rather have the opportunity to become increasingly relevant and meaningful in the pursuit of run-up work.

Finally, we come back to the notion of ableness lifted up in the community perspective of schooling. Ableness has within a strong component of will, versus motivation. There are established patterns of writing that serve to develop will in regards to a subject; no doubt these will have some usefulness within the realm of intentional writing... writing essential to our wellbeing and our continuance upon the upward path of our becoming fully and truly human.

Shifting over to intentional writing's true partner – critical thinking – some other realities come to the fore. A reasonable starting point here is the experientially validate-able reality regarding our thinking:

> *Ultimately, the perspective we hold - where we start our thinking from – determines the path we take, and the direction we move in – what we move towards, what we move away from.*

...a truth as real, and at the very least, as consequential to life on earth, as is gravity. We have a choice. We can choose the perspective we hold – where we start our thinking from – or we can choose to ignore this truth. Either way we are making a choice.

Some other realities come to mind:

> *There are no partial solutions.* Critical thinking today requires the development of one's capacity to see things wholistically and to deal with things systemically... in particular in the way of living systems. This is a real shift from the more common approach

of critical thinking that calls upon the segmenting, fragmenting, analyzing processes of reason. This shift is also necessary such that wisdom, the wisdom of intent, can guide reason.

Virtue – the essence pattern of intent, intended ways of working – is the true source of value. That which distances/disconnects itself from virtue inevitably goes out of existence… be it a product, a process, a people, a country…

We cannot get to value by starting our thinking from economics. We cannot get to value – stay connected to virtue – by starting our thinking from economics. Rather we must start our thinking from virtue/value and generate economics around that… hopefully, at this time, wholistic economics.

Whereas there are no segmented solutions, the breaking things apart with regard to the work before us, the problem solving capacity of science, the scientific method, and other common tools of reason, do not diminish or get dismissed; rather they have the opportunity to become increasingly relevant in the context of today's work… work requiring wholistic approaches and systemic understanding… processes that organize themselves around intended ways of working.

Perhaps worthwhile to remember is that segmented thinking can produce manipulative knowledge – the capacity to shift things in a desired direction, a capacity that can operate in the absence of an ethical question, a question regarding rightness and goodness – right for humanity, good for the whole of life – with the inevitable straying from, going off of, the path of intent… becoming disconnected from virtue, ultimately being of no earthly value.

At first, one may see the realities of today in a not so uplifting light, perhaps even in a somewhat discouraging way. But the ability of clarity, certainty and conviction to generate hope within and among us is not to be underestimated. Experience teaches us of the impossible being done when spirit is accessed and being manifested… spirit brought to life through the seeing of potential. And now is the time of potential, a time for regenerative work; the regeneration of essential systems, of essential processes… regeneration of our ways of working and living… the bringing forth of hope – life giving, spirit lifting hope – that naturally accompanies the seeing of regenerative ways… seeing upward shifts in humanness, increasing congruence with intent. Now this is not a false sense of hope, but rather that which is grounded in an understanding of how we work, an understanding of some essential thinking processes.

Behind our approaches – behind theology, behind ideology, behind business, behind education, etc. – actively at work is philosophy… a guiding philosophy. We have found that a philosophy, organized around the systemic triad of virtue, intentional ethics and potential, enables the development of regenerative approaches, approaches that can be carried forward with the guiding principles of add no infrastructural burden, effectively utilize community resources, and seek processes and pursuits that engender reciprocal nourishment. So there is a path, a way of coming together, that will – through reflection, dialogue, intentional writing and critical thinking, and the leadership that will unfold – allow us to move towards and along the path of intent… the path of bringing the world of our making into congruence with the world of intent.

Seeing the Primary Thrusts of a
Wholistic Country Strategy

For some time I have been engaging in some strategy type questioning regarding "Now is the time"... thinking of strategy in terms of seeing a way along the path, a path of unfolding intent, a way that would bring into focus particular work/thrusts – that which is critical to the aim. Out from that questioning, energized by a conversation with one who is working on business regeneration, these thoughts/conclusions have emerged.

The uniqueness of our work is the central organizing notion of work – work in many forms. Regeneration work – the work of enabling run-up – is the nature of work called for now. Coming from potential is what is required for regeneration work.

The truth, *the perspective you hold – where you start your thinking from – determines the path you take, what you move away from, what you move towards*, acts as a strategy principle, and lifts up the transition process: *what we move away from; what we move towards*.

Three thrusts – points of focus – showed up: A here and now living faith, intentional working community, and business regeneration.... three systemically related focal points of our transitioning process.

> *A HERE AND NOW LIVING FAITH:* A way to live out our faith in the context and reality of today... in reconciling ways that acknowledge our oneness and enable our moving towards wholeness... in ways that are alive in hope – here and now hope.

> *Transition:* Moving away from "because we

are only human"; moving towards "becoming fully and truly human."

INTENTIONAL WORKING COMMUNITY: Ways to come together as community to create processes for growing, educating, developing, and realizing the potential of all the children… community ways that bring the light of hope to all.

> *Transition:* Moving away from pursuing personal advantage/leverage for my child; moving towards seeing and realizing the potential in all children.

BUSINESS REGENERATION: A life of the whole, systemic approach… an intentional way of doing business… working in ways that bring spirit, meaning, and purpose to our endeavors… ways that bring the uplifting buoyancy of hope to ourselves, and to future generations.

> *Transition:* Moving away from extracting through financial manipulation; moving towards value generation sourced in virtue, value generation and realization through product development and systemic offerings… building wholistic economics around that.

These three can be seen as the primary thrusts of a wholistic country strategy that puts us on the path of revitalizing our country.

The transitions – move away from, move towards – reflect both reality and a real way to go forward… provide a way to create the right orientation, a way of creating the void for understanding and spirit to enter, the starting point for the time of now.

The thrusts are about the here and now work, and the shifts we the people need to make in regards to work. More specifically, what we work on, our way of working, and what we work for. It is through work that we develop, that we manifest spirit, that we move towards becoming. The thrusts lift up here and now entry points, as well as some confronting shifts in starting points. That is what is at work here.

Business Regeneration

Ongoing conversations regarding business regeneration have generated additional reflection on my part... reflection that has been energized and organized by the request to make sure we stay product focused, and the emergence of the notion that it is time to increase our interactions... to begin to connect with other folks who have similar leanings towards and like-mindedness regarding business, ways of doing business... time to begin developing a network of folks drawn into this regenerative work – the work of regenerating business.

Business regeneration brings a much more wholistic seeing and systemic process orientation to the work before us... and allows us to see beyond material limitations – the materials involved in recycling/regeneration. So then, here are some thoughts that have emerged around that.

> Business regeneration: a life of the whole, systemic approach... an intentional way of doing business... working in ways that bring spirit, meaning and purpose to our endeavors... ways that bring the uplifting buoyancy of hope to ourselves, to future generations.

As we reflect, it is useful to remember the common law of earthly life, *ultimately, the perspective we hold – where we start our thinking from – determines the path we take, what we move away from, what we move towards.* We can see this at work in regard to a transition principle critical to regenerating business, the transition principle of: Move away from extracting through financial manipulation, and move towards value generation sourced in virtue; value generation and realization through product development and systemic offerings... building economics, wholistic economics, around that.

As we continue our thinking, it is helpful to remember that business is the name we humans give to how we organize to generate and realize value. If we were honeybees we might refer to our hive as our way of organizing to carry out our essential work of pollination and producing life sustaining honey. If we were ants, we might look to hill or nest as a descriptor of our way of organizing to carry out our essential work of soil making… our process of returning organic material to the ground that supports/contains our hill/nest, organic material that through our processing reintegrates into the soil… enriching the soil's capacity to nourish life… a process that nourishes us as well.

Regeneration, regenerative work, requires that we come from – start our thinking from – the perspective of potential rather than from the perspective of problem. It is what we turn to when it is clear that partial solutions lack the resolving power to effectively address the issues before us. It requires wholistic approaches and wholistic understanding.

A life of the whole perspective acknowledges that we are first and foremost living beings and, like all of life's creatures, are inherently dependent upon the vitality and viability of the essential life processes of earth and her essential systemic elements of soil, air and water… a truth and reality not only for ourselves, but for future generations as well.

Coming from a life of the whole perspective, we seek to move towards wholeness… developing products and offerings that are more wholistically generated and reflect a more wholistic understanding of intended ways of working. Reflecting on the systemic elements of soil, air and water brings added imagery to the intent regarding wholeness. Soil, air and water are living domains within which processes critical to the ongoingness of life on earth take place. It is the nature of all living creatures to generate structures that inevitably enter into the working and processes of life itself. As living human beings we are accountable for the structures we bring into existence... an accountability that is enabled by the understanding that all of earth, all of her domains, actively participate in the ongoingness of life... processes critical to our ongoingness. As such, we understand there is no "inactive" isolated domain for the disposal of waste, of the unwanted. "There is no away." Our living in accord with this reality is greatly enabled by seeing the structures we generate as belonging to one of two categories: Those structures that can naturally integrate into the life processes of earth... and those that cannot. For those that can, we pay attention to the rate of introduction to life processes; ensuring that integration capacity is not exceeded. For those that cannot, we create closed systems; ensuring they are prevented from entering the life processes/domains of earth. It is interesting that we can see this naturally at work within earth. We can enrich our images of this by reflecting on life cycles – birth through death and reintegration; and the naturally occurring pockets – closed systems – that contain such things as petroleum. Finally, as seems to be true of wholistic approaches, there is a recognition of the natural necessity for structures, structures related to ongoing existence and wellbeing, no effort to occlude or deny that... but rather a focus on congruence – ways that are congruent with intended ways of working... ways that are right for humanity, good for the whole of life. It is interesting to notice that a life of the whole perspective fully embraces humankind, whereas a human centered perspective commonly, perhaps naturally, does not fully embrace the life of the whole... the whole of which we are a part.

Systemic offerings make real, create a presence of, the stakeholders – those that truly have a stake in the business. In addition to the shareholder, systemic offerings bring to the fore the other stakeholders: employees, customers, community, society, future generations, and life itself. These offerings also bring to light the value, potential and business advantage of an offering systemically structured around virtues, virtues such as carbon neutral, closed systems, recyclable, regenerate-able, perpetual… virtues that allow necessary structures to be generated and used in ways that are harmonious with earth and intended ways of working.

Working Philosophy. Going back to "the perspective we hold" brings up the need to develop a working philosophy… one that emerges from a philosophy that is whole enough, complete enough to deal with today's reality… and one that is practice-able. The living philosophy of potential is such a philosophy. Out from this has emerged a working philosophy… a working philosophy expressed by the systemic triad of *virtue, ethics and potential.* This serves to provide guidance, necessary guidance, for staying on the path of our intent, as well as a source of wisdom in regard to pursuits and actions… true philosophical anchors for going forward.

> We understand virtue to be the ultimate source of value… and the embodiment of the living philosophy of the land – the particular planetary energy field we operate within.

> Ethics – that which requires an understanding of intended ways of working; and allows us to pursue and act in accord with the right and good… right for the one; good for the whole.

> Potential – coming from potential, realizing potential, taking things to essence as a means of understanding intent, intended ways of working.

We can see this systemic triad at work in working on petroleum; seeing "perpetual products" as the essential virtue, creating those products in carbon neutral ways, employing recycling/regenerating processes, and developing necessary

126

closed systems.

Guiding principles. These emanate from the working philosophy and provide further freedom and guidance to go forward. A systemic set of guiding principles in regard to this regenerating work has emerged:

> Add no infrastructural burden.
>
> Effectively use community resources.
>
> Seek processes and pursuits that engender reciprocal nourishment.

Reciprocal nourishment comes to life as we add the whole of the stakeholders to our imagery and strategy... a process that lifts up necessary shifts in some of our essential processes (education for example), shifts that themselves require reciprocal nourishment to come about.

Faith. Perhaps a useful closing thought is in regard to faith. Reflecting on faith, what we have faith in, and what we can put our faith in, are useful reflective questions as one takes on a pursuit, especially ones such as this. Bolstered by experience we have faith that if we maintain our intent, our commitment to this path, we will not only see that which we previously could not see, but also see and understand that which we need to continue in order to progress along this path of intent. One "seeing and understanding" that has emerged from this work is that this pursuit is not so much dependent upon new invention, but rather lends itself to a systemic integration of existing technologies. An experienced reality that is an ongoing source of hope... hope in our seeing that this can really be done... and it can be done now.

Wholistic Country Strategy Realities

Every so often, some ongoing issues within our country evoke some thoughts about country strategy, in particular the absence of, and need for, a wholistic country strategy. This time, however, the focus is more about approaches and processes... our common ways of addressing issues versus the issues themselves. The issues that evoked the thoughts are our debt and the economy. Reflecting on these issues lifted up the limitations in our common approaches and processes. A few words about the issues might be helpful grounding for considering our approaches and processes.

Looking first at debt reduction/bonds, we see some interesting things. Recently, the S & P has lowered our rating. Our bonds are still a favored place for investment, sufficiently favored that there has been no apparent demand for significant increase in regards to the interest we need to pay. In one sort of way, investors, including the likes of China, seem to be saying that the U.S. is still a good bet; perhaps one of the best bets on a relative basis. And it is probably not too much of a stretch to imagine that folks have some faith, and perhaps a lot of hope/wish, that the U.S. will get its act together... and maybe even some hope that the U.S. will lead the world out of its dilemma. On the other hand, we are being "offered" really cheap money that, under other circumstances, would allow us to wisely invest in that which is critical to our ongoing wellbeing. However it does not seem likely that we could take advantage of this opportunity.

Juxtaposed to our debt issue is the issue of sluggish economy/market behavior. There have been some significant swings in the market; and some expectation of a downward trend. And there is some, shall we say, hoarding of cash by corporations. Which along with market expectations indicates some reluctance to invest. Jobs, the lack of jobs, is a real and growing concern. There is some evidence of declining wages and benefits, some sense we are bringing the pattern of overseas investment home with us – in the form of lower wage job creation. It is not difficult to imagine that debt reduction, budget cuts, will result in further loss of jobs. Our economy, and much of the world's economy, is consumer driven… highly leveraged in this direction. Much of what is happening does not lend itself to real increases in consumer spending. Thus potential for economic growth (a keystone for investment) is lacking. To paraphrase Henry Ford: No buying power, no buyers, no sales, no revenue.

Meanwhile we continue to be hindered by some realities regarding our approaches and processes… approaches and processes that we seem to have a fair level of commitment and attachment to. Two of the most common, and their limitations are:

> We are severely limited by the segmented reasoning present in, common to, problem solving approaches.

> We are stymied – in a see-saw, circular sort of way – by the rigid, disenabling limitations of existing ideologies.

What adds to our dilemma is that neither of these, separately or working together, have the resolving power to create a sustainable upward shift in our country… nor with and for the people. As implied before, this is not intended criticism, rather just a statement of what is – what is, given the natural working and inherent nature of these approaches and processes. Now we know from experience that little if anything is more debilitating than uncertainty. Given the limitations of our current ways and path, we can be certain that uncertainty will thrive.

There is, however, a way, an upward path… a way and path

that requires a shift in the starting point of our thinking... a shift to starting our thinking from a life of the whole perspective... a life of the whole, systemic approach which includes some serious reflection and dialogue on intentional purpose... the intentional purpose of the institutions, systems and processes critical to our way of working... things such as business, education, governmentat all levels, banking, legal systems, ethical processes, etc.

As I paused to end this note, I began to imagine asking Mere Mere and my mother, for wise counsel in this matter. Imagining their voices, I could hear them say, in a reprimanding sort of way: "Any path, any strategic path that reduces our intended humanness is in reality no path at all." Or, put another way, any strategic pursuit, if it is to be real, needs to move us in the direction of working for all children, all children in the world...

Thy Will Be Done

O, Lord,
It is our wish, our most heartfelt wish,
to do Thy will, not my will.

As we seek to do Thy will,
shower us with, and help us to be open to
the grace and love we need:

> *To resist surrendering to the comfortable,*
> *to worldly opinion, to our image of what should be...*

> *To have the eyes and the wisdom*
> *to see the right and good – what is intended...*

> *And to know when my will, not Thy will is directing us.*

Grant us our wish, so that
through your love and intention
we can be and become instruments of your work...
of your will on this earth... at this time.

As human beings we have within us the ableness to be both energizing and energized... and perhaps more deeply within, lies the potential to be organized by spirit... spirit entering, spirit manifesting. We have before us the work of advancing our humanness, work calling for accessing and manifesting spirit... a process of coming from virtue, taking up essential work, and by so doing, moving towards becoming fully and truly human... continuing along the path of intent, a path of spirit, of spirit being manifested through work... work and role that reflects our inherent instrumentality... a way of spirit being enfolded into life... a process essential to the eternalizing of life.

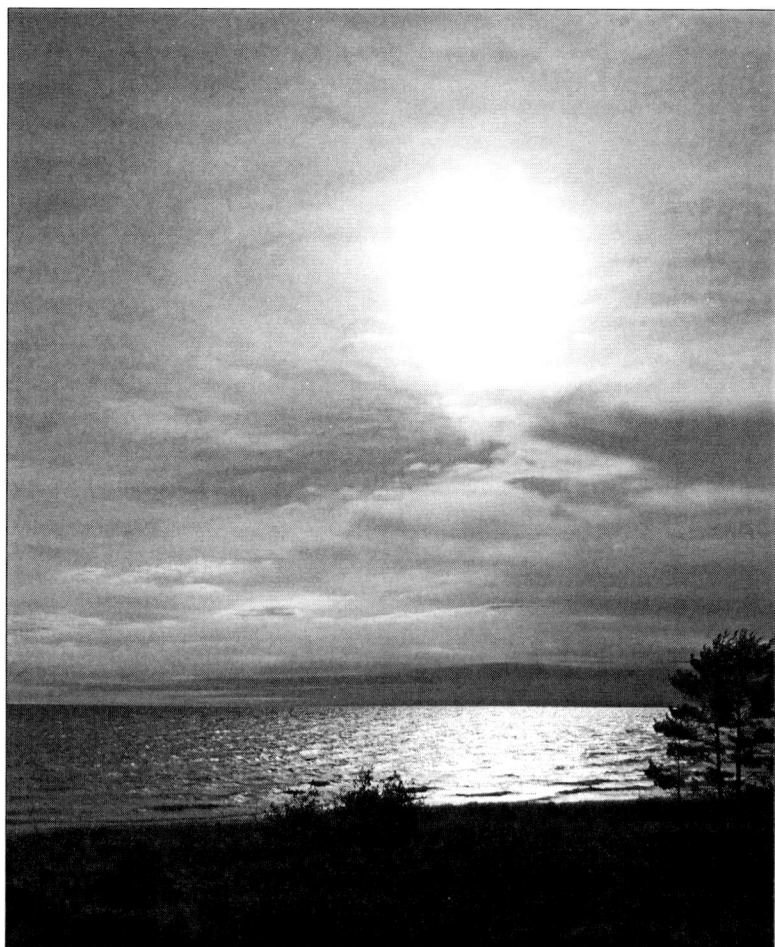

Volume Three…

BUILDING A
GOING FORWARD FAITH

Taking up the Work of Moving towards Wholeness…
Taking up Pursuits that Work for All Children

On Being Disconnected

Early this fall, I was camping with my son in the Wind River Mountains. I have been doing this for over thirty years. Lately, and in particular this year, I have come to recognize that I am approaching the end of the trail with regard to the rigors of this trip. With that in mind, I decided that I would leave the comfort of my tent – nights often fall below freezing at this time of the year – and go out and observe the late night sky… that time of night that reminds us of the old saying, "It is always darkest before the dawn."

Over the years I have come to see and appreciate how different the night sky looks at this time… not only in terms of where particular stars are, but also for the experiencing of the vastness and depth of the universe, uniquely present at this time. This year I was camped in a spot that was especially suited to late night appreciation of the sky. My tent was set up in the open, about thirty feet or so from the edge of a lake… an edge that itself dropped sharply into the water.

On the particular night of memory I crawled from my tent – one man tents require such an exit – pushed myself erect and walked towards the edge of the lake. As I approached the lake, I was struck by its calmness, an icy calmness, a smoothness of surface unlike any I had ever witnessed. Off to my right, I noticed the bright reflection of a star; and as I squared myself to better see Mount Victor – the organizing landmark for our campsite – I saw before me, at my feet, the Big Dipper… upside down, with its mouth open to me… an opening that created within me a compelling sense of being drawn towards, of being invited in… a real impulse of stepping off the edge… of jumping joyfully into the waiting arms of the Big Dipper. As I paused to contemplate this, I looked up and saw the Big Dipper sitting, perfectly balanced on the top of Mount Victor; Victor not being reflected upon the water given the level of darkness and the absence of light beyond starlight. As I stood before this scene, the natural amazement of "Wow!" continued to deepen… to penetrate within, innerly reaching depths not previously experienced. And, as is not uncommon for me, a process of reflective questioning began… a questioning of what is this… this which I am seeing and so deeply experiencing… a questioning that eventually brought forth clarity, a clarity of seeing, of thought, that this is beauty… an expression and experience of beauty present in the creation, a beauty possible only through the Source of creation… a true connection to the Source beyond anything I had known.

 Throughout the trip, I did live up to my intent, rousing myself from my tent to breathe in and feast my eyes on that which appeared before me. And on several of those nights, I did see the reflection of the Big Dipper in the water… but a much fuzzier picture than that night, a night when the reflection on the polished mirror of the lake was clearer, more intense than the actual image of the dipper against the darkest of skies. So while I did not have a repeat of that forever special night, I did have another late night experience, a very different experience, a very intense experience. A few nights after the night of beauty, I found myself fully awake, preparing myself to leave my tent and embrace the late night sky. As I lay there, some images entered, imposing themselves on my mind… a mind occupied with expectations of beauty. Beauty expectations were quickly and forcefully displaced with a plethora of ever changing, fast moving, increasingly alive images… images I began to experience as a cacophony of image and voice… an overwhelming crescendo of negativity, of coarse energy… of faces and voices urging me, compelling me to purchase, to do, to hate, to follow them, and on and on… an intensity that kept increasing, penetrating further within me… a suffocating grasp that I could not turn off. From a growing sense of helplessness and fear, an inner voice began to cry out: "No!...No!...No!.." As breathing became more difficult, I, with anxious vigor, unzipped my tent, and rolled out onto the ground. As I lay there looking up at the sky, breathing began to return; and slowly the unnerving voices and images began to diminish and disappear. At last I could freely breathe again, fully inhale the crisp fresh air. I got up and walked to the edge of the lake. The dipper was fully visible in the sky. The lake was gently rippled; a fuzzy but reassuring image lay upon it. And as is my pattern, that which I had innerly experienced was the source of a questioning, a prayerful questioning common to this time of potential... a process of reflecting and contemplating out from which emerged a clear answer... that this was an experience of hell – of being disconnected from the Source, the Source of all, of the whole of creation.

After returning home, some ongoing reflection and interaction has brought forth some additional seeing and understanding... seeing and understanding relevant to this time of potential... a time for moving towards wholeness, away from that which divides... a time for working for all children, all children in the world.

Beauty, the inner experience of the beauty of creation, works to keep us connected to the Source, to that which is beyond ourselves, the Source of each and all. It works to remind us that we are not the source. It moves us in a direction of a more wholistic seeing and honoring of the Source... a wholeness that embraces the creation side of the Source, the intent and intended ways of working that lie within the whole of creation... within ourselves, within the whole of life... an intentionality that is frequently not present in our ideologies and pursuits.

Moving towards wholeness, within and among ourselves, will require a more wholistic seeing and understanding of the Source… a coalescence of intent… intent and intended ways of working as lifted up in the word and the works… a coalescence made possible through the intuition of wholeness… the intuition we call upon to access wisdom, the wisdom of intent. Moving towards wholeness is much more akin to a path of beauty, than the path depicted in my experience of hell.

Terry P. Anderson
September, 2012

That was Then; Now is Now

In the beginning,

> *our very first act of disobedience*

>> *was to interfere with the intended working of the world…*

In the beginning, at the earliest of human times… through the intentional act of the Creator… there emerged from the earth, a people – a living people of earth. The people enjoyed an unending abundance, constant happiness, and real peace. A harmony existed among all the creatures of earth.

At the start of the beginning, the intention of the Creator was made known. The Creator put forth instructions or laws by which the people were to live in community. Now the people, being unique among life's creatures, could choose to obey or not to obey the Creator's laws. The people, by intent, were endowed with free will – and as such were not subject to the automatic behavior and obedience practiced by the other creatures of earth. Somewhere along the way, temptation became ever more present. Succumbing to this temptation, the people chose to act from themselves, rather than live in accord with the Creator's instructions.

The people became increasingly knowledgeable, but decreasingly wise. More and more they used their knowledge to serve themselves; less and less regard did they have for the Creator's intention. As time passed – as they progressed along their chosen path – the people began to experience illness, sorrow, war, strife, woe and emptiness… the opposite of the beginning. Earth, the very home of life itself, became threatened.

That was then…

Now is now…

The past is past…

The future is yet to unfold. Now is the time to uncover a
new path – a new way of being.

> The people are beginning to awaken.
> Conscience is being stirred to life.
> Love is seeking to enter.
> Hearts are opening themselves to wisdom.
> Intuition is coming into play.

There is a growing sense of a calling…

> A calling to reclaim our heritage…
>> our heritage of peace and wholeness…
> A calling to fulfill our role…
>> our role in advancing humanness.

An ethic is striving to emerge…
An ethic for living wisely on this earth…
An ethic born from essential truths…

> … the truth of our being a people of earth.
> … the truth of our shared humanness.
> … the truth of our being members of the community of life.
> … the truth of our common Source.
> … the truth of our calling to become fully and truly human.
> … the truth that all are called, and each may choose.

Now is the time of potential…

Now is the time of potential, a time for moving towards
wholeness, away from that which divides… a time for tak-

ing up pursuits that move us in the direction of that which works for all children, all children in the world.

As we take up the work before us, the work of advancing our humanness, the work called for, the necessary work of this time, it is important that we hold in mind and reflect upon the common law of earthly life… a useful orientation and understanding for sustaining the integrity of our efforts, for our being faithful to the work, and for ensuring/enabling our progression along the path of intent, the path of our potential to become fully and truly human… the path of hope, hope for all children, hope for the whole of life – to which we, through the intent of the Source, clearly belong. The common law of earthly life:

Ultimately, the perspective we hold,
where we start ourthinking from,
determines the path we take, the direction we move in,
what we move towards, what we move away from.

The work of moving towards wholeness, away from that which divides, requires a perspective of wholeness… wholeness of Source, wholeness of intent, wholeness with regard to life… wholeness with regard to the here and unfolding now.

Taking up the work, developing serious intent with regard to the work before us, requires particular seeing and understanding… seeing and understanding related to the building of going forward faith… an understanding of and openness to that which is striving to emerge… a seeing and understanding which itself is developed through reflection and dialogue… reflecting and dialoguing that calls upon and works through intuition, the intuition of wholeness… reflecting and dialoguing that bring clarity to work – to our called work, the unfolding work of ourselves, of our commu-

141

nities, of our country.

The ongoing work of making visible the path of potential, our potential to become fully and truly human, has and continues to bring forth images and understandings related to wholeness... wholeness of philosophy, wholeness of perspective, wholeness of life, and increasing clarity with regard to wholeness of Source. What follows is a series of writings, a collection of thoughts that have emerged from this work... thoughts related to this unfolding work, thoughts that, through reflection and dialogue, will hopefully enable the development of the nature of faith required for sustaining our commitment to the path and to the work.

Reflecting on the Sorting Out
Process of Wisdom

The sorting out process of wisdom is the process we engage in when we are seeking to see and embrace the whole... it is the struggle we willfully undertake to bring forth a deeper more wholistic understanding of essential truth.

The sorting out process of wisdom is perhaps less familiar than the much more common process of reason... reason being the process of developing and engaging in argument, a winning argument... the aim of which is the structuring condensation of knowledge.

The processes of wisdom and reason share an experiencing of struggle... perhaps the struggle related to wisdom is more akin to willfully opening our arms to more fully embrace truth... whereas the struggle with regard to reason is more akin to arm wrestling your brother.

The aim of sorting out is to gain clarity with regard to the possible, and to potential. Whereas, given the reality of our existence, of the way of life on earth, much is possible; our work at this time requires pursuit of and congruence with the intentional. It is through seeing potential that we can move towards being and becoming intentional, intentional people of earth, intentional people of life.

Current Reality:
The Loss of Our Humanness…
A Real Risk of Today

Note:
Useful grounding is holding in mind the common law of earthly life, a way of our working that is as common and active as gravity:

> *Ultimately, the perspective we hold, where we start our thinking from, determines the path we take, the direction we move in, what we move towards, what we move away from.*

Useful orientation is remembering that:

> *There is a Source… we are not the source.*
> *There is intent and intended ways of working that emanate from and through the Source.*
> *Earth was created for life to have a place to enter into the working of the universe.*
> *We are intentionally, not accidently, created as living, as human, as beings… as living human beings.*

The useful notion of a central forming core:

> *A central forming core, the organizing thought base out from which flows and unfolds a multitude of thoughts, is a key to seeing and understanding what is at work, and for seeing intended ways of working as well.*

The central forming core of our humanness is the virtues of faith, hope and love… virtues that can be seen at work from the perspective of existence and from the perspective of essence… as the foundation of our humanness, and from our potential to be and become fully and truly human.

Faith, Hope and Love from the Perspective of Existence

As living human beings on earth, particular manifestations of faith, hope and love come to us and through us from realities of existence... from that which it is necessary and natural for humans to seek and create. We see this at work with regard to faith. A reality of life, of human life, is that we are not self-generating. From generation to generation there is a need to rely on the knowledge of previous generations. From generation to generation we cannot start over – go back to ground zero. This reliance carries over to other arenas as well. There is a need to rely upon others in regards to, is the water safe to drink, the air safe to breathe, the food okay to consume... a reliance regarding, is this bridge safe to cross, the plane safe to fly, etc.... a reliance and reality that transcend our deepest sense of independence; of our being able to take care of ourselves – to take care of our own... a reality of connectedness that is increasingly so, rather than diminishingly so... a more and more inescapable reality.

Emerging from the reality of reliance, at the core of faith – existence-based faith – is *integrity*... the need for, the expectation of integrity. We expect integrity within and from those to whom we look for knowledge. We also expect and require (a necessity for maintaining our humanness) integrity within the processes essential to our wellbeing... educating our children, all children; governing, banking, producing, transporting, etc., an integrity that carries over to the systems we construct to serve and support essential human life processes. It is common, as we reflect on integrity, to bring forth the notion of trust. Whereas trust is an element within integrity, integrity carries a more wholistic, all-encompassing sense of completeness. Integrity involves wholeness, the maintaining of wholeness, the basis for moving towards wholeness.

As integrity diminishes, so too does faith, a central character of our humanness, diminish. So too does that which we

put faith in. Life becomes unnecessarily difficult, discon-
certing. Human spirit turns towards coarser and coarser
energies. Instinctual urges become more directing –
become that which leads our thinking. Self-centeredness
gains strength. Divisiveness flourishes… and on and on.

Hope, a systemic element of our humanness, is a naturally
occurring process for human beings living on earth…. to
hope, to have hope, to see hope, is an inherent aspect of our
experience of life. At the core of hope lies *progression*. The
presence of, the opportunity for, and the possibility of progression is found at the core of hope. We see this at work
in our natural desire to move up levels of existence, within
our notions of a better future for our children. It is present
in the notion of our not waking up each day wanting to be
a lesser person, but rather a better person… and it is present
in some practical realities of existence – the need to earn a
living, to support ourselves, our families, our communities.

Hope is a common initiator of reflection… of inner reflecting and questioning regarding to whom, to what, do we look
for hope… a nature of seeking and questioning that is
essential to sustaining our intended humanness.

Love, that aspect of our central forming core, is manifested
and experienced as *compassion*. With regard to existence –
to realities of our living – the particular manifestation of
love is the *compassion of caring for*… of the able caring for
the unable. The compassion of caring for reflects the reality that there are times in our life when we are not self-sustaining; self-sustaining being related to self-supporting, but
a more wholistic notion. We can readily see this at work in
the early stages of life, and the latter stages of life. And with
a bit of reflection, we see it at work in the times between.

The ongoingness of human society requires ableness with
regard to self-sustaining. The compassion of caring for
seems to – by necessity and intent – encompass both the

need for being self-sustaining and those times when we are not able to be so.

Now, given that we are in the time of moving towards wholeness, away from that which divides – a time for wholistic seeing and understanding, a time for wholistic approaches – wholistic thought patterns are emerging that enable wholeness – wholeness of thought and the seeing of the underlying processes of wholeness. An example of a wholistic thought pattern depicting the central forming core of human existence – the foundational platform of humanness is this:

Pattern Of Intent Regarding
The Sustaining of Our Humanness

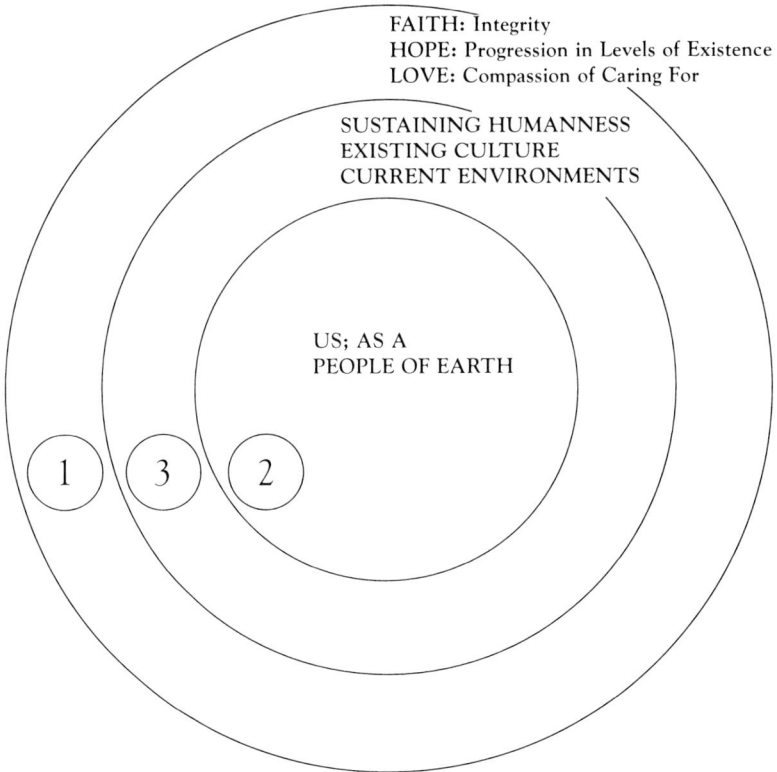

FAITH: Integrity
HOPE: Progression in Levels of Existence
LOVE: Compassion of Caring For

SUSTAINING HUMANNESS
EXISTING CULTURE
CURRENT ENVIRONMENTS

US; AS A
PEOPLE OF EARTH

1

3

2

1 – 2 – 3 PROCESS. The 1 – 2 – 3 PROCESS is the intend-

ed process; the intent being that we draw faith, hope and love through ourselves (remembering that we are not the source of these virtues) and bring them forth into the environments we engage (e.g., community, work, school, etc.), establishing cultures(s) that work to sustain our humanness.

<u>3 –2 – – – 1 PROCESS</u> This process being a process where the culture begins to define us… moves us in the direction of being a slave to it, and away from the Source… more in the direction of a dotted line connection to the Source – a sometimes connection.

A few thoughts that seem relevant in this regard:
> *Each and all emerge from a common Source.*
> *The essence of the Source is love.*
> *It is through the intent of the Source that we are*
>   *created as living human beings.*

Understanding this allows us to intuitively see humanness as significant – significant to the Source, and that which we should hold as significant. With regard to love, essential love, we are not self-sustaining… not in the beginning, not at the end, nor during the time between; thus the necessity of the 1 – 2 – 3 PROCESS; and the hazard to each and all of the 3 – 2 – – – 1 PROCESS, a hazard not only to humanity, but to the intended unfolding of the Source.

A few thoughts with regard to some chief features of our current culture: Our existence-based culture commonly expresses a possessional, positional, functional character. Possessional – all about stuff; positional – societal position; functional – all about doing; what we do, what we can do, a general attachment to busyness, etc. It is beyond the scope, and the hoped for intent of this writing, to delve deeply or even casually into the issues of our current culture. I would hope that what has been written would provide sufficient imagery to see what is at work, the direction we, without conscientious intervention, are moving in. Perhaps it is sufficient to say that culture – that system of values that we put in place – works. When that culture is a reflection of intended ways of working, we move in a particular direction; when that culture is a reflection more of our wishes than of intent, we move in particular directions. Hopefully this writing enables more conscious choices on our part… the nature of choices our humanness requires.

We started this writing by lifting up the realness of the risk to our humanness – the risk to humanity, the hazard to the unfolding intent of the Source. Along the way we brought forth a depiction – a wholistic thought pattern – of intent and intended ways of working. The intent of the writing (more clear to the writer now, than at the beginning of the writing) is to provide some essential grounding regarding what is at work, and intended ways of working… a depiction of current reality, with the hope that seeing what is at work will help us break away from debilitating attachments – those attachments that move us in the direction of diminishing humanness, attachments that themselves can become addictions.

Healthy Working Humanizing Economy

Given the current reality focus of this writing, it seems necessary to put forth some thoughts with regard to a common, often prevailing notion within our human society that the most pressing problem we face is the economy… a robust economy being that which we look to for hope, that which we put faith in. Thus some thoughts organized around a healthy working humanizing economy; humanizing in the sense that it does not diminish nor degrade our humanness… and most intentionally would advance our humanness. It is useful as we consider this subject to remind ourselves of the common law of earthly life. Thus starting our thinking from economy/economics takes us down a distinctly different path than that lifted up by starting our thinking from virtue/value – especially the virtue/values at the core of our humanness. And too, we notice that holding the perspective of potential brings to the fore that which is invisible to the perspective of problem.

Most simply we would hold virtue/value as the central forming core and develop economics around that, an organizing that would both reflect intent/intended ways of working and the necessity for reciprocally nourishing economics to sustain our existence and to realize our potential.

Wholistic Economics

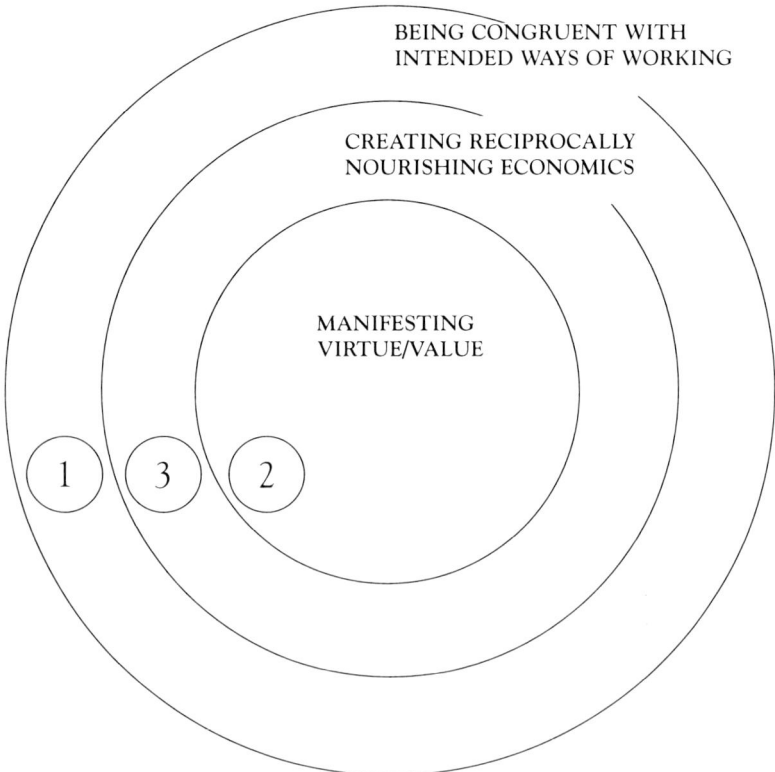

BEING CONGRUENT WITH
INTENDED WAYS OF WORKING

CREATING RECIPROCALLY
NOURISHING ECONOMICS

MANIFESTING
VIRTUE/VALUE

1   3   2

As we reflect on this wholistic thought pattern, we can see the universal values of humanness imbedded within our ways of working, and reflected within our product offering, with our offering being organized around the essence virtue of petroleum as being perpetual – a source for perpetual products.

With a bit of reflection, we can see those times when our ways of working and product offerings are a reflection of intent, of intentional ethics... and those times when one or both reflect diminishment or degradation of our humanness.

Conscious choice of path and conscientious decisions along the path are especially critical at this time... a time of hazard, a time of great potential. Both choice and decisions can be enabled by the motherly command:

Do not move in directions that diminish,
reduce or degrade humanness.

This is not the end of the story. Rather it is a charcoal sketch of the ground for the unfolding story of a people who willfully choose to continue to advance their humanness... to take up the work, our intended work.

What Now Needs to be Made Real...
Now is the Time for Taking up the Work,
*The work of bringing forth an upward shift
in our humanness...
The next step along our intended path of
becoming fully and truly human.*

Note:
As was true for our reflections on current reality, it is useful
to hold in mind the common law of earthly life...

> *Ultimately, the perspective we hold, where we start our
> thinking from, determines the path we take, the direction
> we move in, what we move towards, what we move
> away from.*

Some useful orientations:

> *There is a Source, a common Source of each and all...
> of the whole of all.*
> *We are not the source, but rather are intended
> instruments.*
> *There is intent and intended ways of working that
> emanate from and through the Source.*
> *Earth was created for life to have a place to enter into the
> working of the universe... into the whole of cre-
> ation.*
> *We are, by intent, created as living human beings.
> It is our humanness that is the source of our
> uniqueness; the uniqueness that we bring
> into life and the life processes of earth.*

Faith, Hope and Love from the Perspective of Essence.

Through love all things are possible (MK10:27; 1JN4:16). Love
elevates, creating within us that which we cannot bring
about on our own. It is through love that that which we
bring forth is beyond that which is considered possible...

152

the previously unimaginable. It is through love that we are able to join in the bringing forth of the unfolding image of the Source... the bringing forth of a world that reflects the intent and intended ways of working of the Source.

It is love, the essence pattern of love manifested through Christ on earth, that makes the next advancement of our humanness possible... the essence pattern of caring about, caring about the larger whole... a pattern that holds within, the previous pattern of caring for, but emerges as a deeper, more wholistic expression of that essential truth. It is the *compassion of caring about* that makes possible our taking up pursuits that work for all children, all children in the world... work that has "my and mine" enfolded within, but is a more wholistic expression of the intent of the Source... work itself that requires a life of the whole perspective.

Reflecting further, Christ came, not to displace nor to diminish the Source, but rather to reconnect us to the Source... to re-establish proper relatedness to the Source... a relatedness disturbed by our first act of disobedience, our interfering in the intended way of working of the world... a relatedness that would allow and enable the return to the path of intent, the path of our potential... the path and way of our becoming fully and truly human. Christ, by word and works, called attention to the Source – the Father... pointing out that *Only the Father is good, I came to do the work of my Father; I was sent*, etc. (LK18:19; JN4:34; JN17:18).

The central forming core of Christian religion is salvation, our being saved... an organizing core dealing with the returning aspect of humanity – our longing to return, the returning of Christ... a central forming core that emerges from a human centered perspective... a perspective that at times can occlude a more wholistic seeing and understanding of the creation – its intent and intended ways of working... a perspective that, through temptation, may engender the not uncommon expression, "I am saved; he is coming; what happens to earth, what we do to life and essential life processes of earth, is irrelevant;" a tempting start point for our thinking that often carries with it the notion of earth not being created for life to enter into the working of the universe, but rather solely for ourselves, for us to do with as we please... a start point that engenders the illusion that we are separate from, independent of, life and of essential life processes.

Now, at this time of potential, it is necessary to more fully embrace the going forward commandments Christ gave us: the eternal commandment – *Love God* (MK12:30) – and the new commandment – *Love one another as I have loved you* (JN13:34). The eternal commandment intended to be ongoing, ongoing forever. At this time, we see within the eternal commandment, a life of the whole perspective... our living in ways congruent with intent and intended ways of working with regard to the whole of life on earth – the manifested works of the Source.

With regard to the new commandment, we see the essential truths of the previous – *Love thy neighbor as thyself* (MT22:39) – enfolded within and emerging as a deeper, more wholistic manifestation in the new – *Love one another as I have loved you*... an inclusive love, that makes possible our taking up pursuits that work for all children, all children in the world... pursuits that include our children, but embrace all children... and by necessity, the whole of life on which the future of all children depends.

The intent to reconnect us to the Source shows up in Christ's teaching regarding prayer: *Our Father, who art in heaven, hallowed be thy name, thy kingdom come, thy will be done on earth, as it is in heaven... lead us not into temptation, but deliver us from evil* (MT6:9-13). To be connected to the

154

Source is to be led by Thy will, not my will… and clearly there is an intent for that regarding the here – on this earth – and the unfolding now; an image that is further enriched by seeing this prayer in the light of prophecy – a statement of intent, the intent of the Source… a serious intent of the Source… Thy will being at the core of all serious intent… that which Christ displayed in his work on earth… that which is to be present in our work on earth.

Contemplating his departure, Christ wonders whether or not there will be people of faith when he returns (LK18:8)… people of faith being the fruit of his labors, that which he can point to with regard to his work, that which he was sent for, that which he could point to the Father as having accomplished what was intended by his coming to earth, that which came about through his saying "Yes" to the cup before him (LK22:42)… people of faith being those who had faith in the intent and intended ways of working of the Source, and were seriously working at developing congruence with that intent, a necessity for today, a necessity to the ongoing intended unfolding.

Now is the time of potential, the time for accessing and manifesting spirit… the time for realizing the potential made possible through the work of Christ… a time for enfolding the truths of salvation into a more wholistic expression and manifestation of the truths made visible and accessible through Christ… truths essential to the next advancement of our humanness… a time for taking up the work, the Thy will work, the intentional work of the Source… a time for moving towards our being and becoming intentional people.

The end of time is the beginning of potential… a time of revitalization, of bringing new life to earth's people, and to earth herself… an era of potential noted by an upward shift in faith, hope and love: the central forming core of our humanness, the essence pattern of intent. Here in the unfolding now, the virtues of faith, hope and love emerge as:

Faith: Faith in the intent and intended ways of working of the Source.

Hope: Progression in our humanness, a step change along our path of becoming fully and truly human.

Love: Compassion of caring about, caring about the whole – the whole of life, and all children in the world.

Pattern of Intent Regarding
The Advancing of Our Humaness

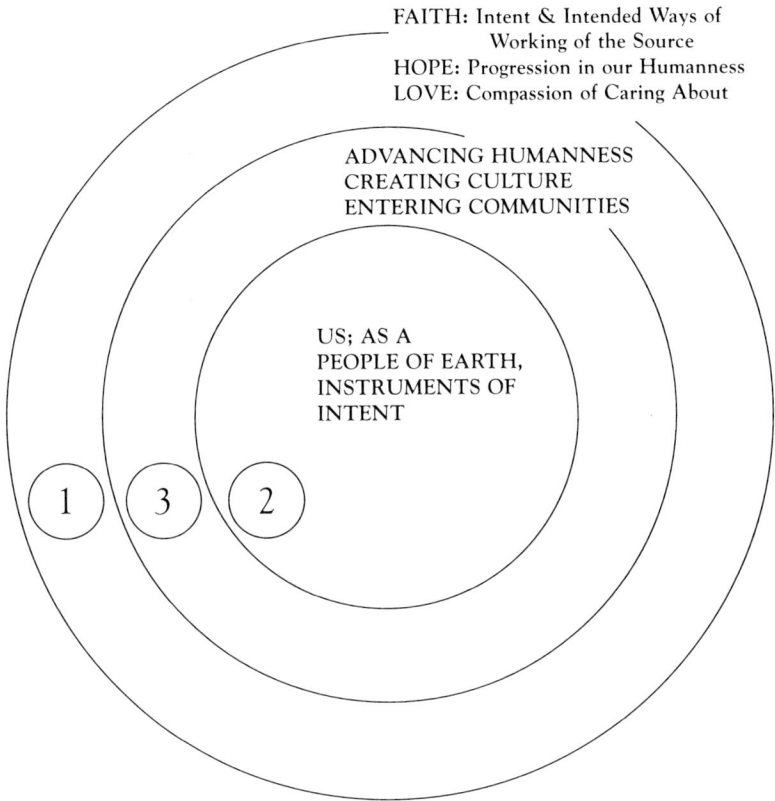

FAITH: Intent & Intended Ways of
Working of the Source
HOPE: Progression in our Humanness
LOVE: Compassion of Caring About

ADVANCING HUMANNESS
CREATING CULTURE
ENTERING COMMUNITIES

US; AS A
PEOPLE OF EARTH,
INSTRUMENTS OF
INTENT

1   3   2

Intentionally Moving Towards
Faith, Hope and Love

At this time of potential, we see faith, hope and love as virtues... virtues out from which values emerge, values being particular expressions of virtue appropriate to the situation, and that which keep us on the path of becoming fully and truly human. In this context:

– Faith: The word that seems to best capture the core or essence is *intentionality*. Having faith in our ableness to live from and in congruence with *intent, intended ways of working*. Inherent within is potential – potential not yet realized... a potential for intentionality, for being intentional, for creating intentional community. Faith bolstered by the Gospels (*birds of the air, flowers of the field* (MT6:26-28)) and some shifting in how we are approaching issues and pursuits. We have faith that we can access that which is inherently possible within and move in the direction of intentionality... living more in accord with intended ways... not just sometimes, but ongoingly through time. A faith strengthened by, and in reality made real by the unfolding understanding of intent and intended ways of working... an understanding that is organizing and organized by the living philosophy of potential... a philosophy whole enough, complete enough to enable the called for shift... a philosophy that, through writings and dialoguing, is both accessible and practice-able. Further we have faith that if we maintain our commitment to intent we will be given all we need to move along the path of human potential... the path of becoming fully and truly human.

– Hope: Here the word, *becoming*, seems to describe the essence or core. Becoming carries with it the character of progression, *progression through the advancement of our humanness*... an advancement that encompasses the realities of existence but indexes more towards being and spirit than the possessional/positional focus of the current culture. Hope will increase as we move in the direction of pursuing that which will work for all children, all children in the world... work that brings forth work of the heart as a means for us as a country becoming more intentional... increasing our ableness to live from essential virtues... bringing forth a more wholistic expression of the essential forming virtue(s) of our country. Central and critical to making hope real – actively present in the process – is the willful freeing of ourselves from artificial boundaries. The requirement of will becomes clear when we recognize that the current – current culture, current valuing of faith, hope and love – represents artificial boundaries to our becoming... boundaries that interfere with the developing of serious intent, and the taking up of the work before us... a situation not unlike that of Mary and her time.

– Love: Here, as in the current, compassion is at the core. However it is the *compassion of equality, the compassion of caring about*, that emerges now... the compassion of caring about the larger whole, the whole of life, the whole of humanity... equality in the sense of potential, each and all having potential, a gift to bring forth... an equality that rings true for communities/countries – the smallest whole at this time of potential. Seeing country as the smallest whole in the context of equality brings forth many images of our country's work and role in the world... work and role that is organized around pursuits that work for all children in the world. Central to both sustaining and advancing our humanness is the willful process of seeing the world through the eyes of another. The compassion of equality reflects that pattern of love necessary for the shift called for at this time... an essence pattern of love requiring community/country as the smallest whole... an equality that uses openness, receptivity and inclusivity as essential processes, processes enabled by the understanding that there is virtue/good in all. We can see the potential in these processes to enable our transcending artificial boundaries, boundaries that not only interfere with our becoming; but boundaries that serve to divide, to move us away from wholeness.

Pausing reflectively for a bit, brings further imagery and understanding. We can see in the working of faith, hope and love as values (current/existence), a real hazard of attachment. There is a natural attraction and pull – not unlike gravity – to stay within, not venture out of the boundaries of existence – existence-based values – a comfort-seeking pull to live in and from the existence values… an attraction and pull that lends itself to attachment… an attachment that we can become enslaved by, owned by… an enslavement that holds us within existence; within the possessional, positional, functional aspects of existence… a gravitational pull strong enough to keep us from engaging essence, potential – the becoming side of life, that aspect of life that deals with spirit, spirit manifesting, fulfilling intent. Given the reinforcing, strengthening character of our culture, religions, etc., it is necessary to engage the process of transcending… transcending the existence values/cultural values, a transcending made visible through the intuition of wholeness… transcending versus rejecting, because rejecting, like attachment, carries with it the hazard of being enslaved, of being captured by.

We have long understood this process of becoming to be a will process… a process calling for the accessing of will… thus the attention to Thy will. With the clarity regarding our functional culture, we can see the necessity to engage will such that being is created from above (versus from existence energies)… a being organized by spirit, manifesting spirit… a being seeking congruence with Thy will, intent, intended ways of working… a being seeking to become an intentional being.

Wholeness of Source

There is a Source, a common Source of all, a Source out from which emerges the whole of creation, the ongoing, unfolding creation.

Within and out from the Source emerges intent, intended ways of working, intent with regard to the whole of creation, of which we are a part.

It is both reasonable and intuitively obvious that if we are to move towards wholeness, the perspective we hold needs to embrace wholeness... wholeness versus a fragmented part, a fragmented thought.

The ultimate start point – the anchor point of our process – is the Source, seeing the Source wholistically, wholistically embracing the Source. Developing a seeing and understanding that encompasses the whole of the Source is essential for the particular advancement in humanness called for at this time; a partial perspective is insufficient for the work at hand.

Wholeness of Source both enables and demands wholeness with regard to intent, intended ways of working... wholeness with regard to the hereafter and the here and unfolding now... wholeness with regard to our longing to return and our yearning to become... wholeness with regard to the intentionality present within life, within its systems and processes, within ourselves as living human beings.

Key for us at this time is some clarity regarding the contrast between sufficiently whole, sufficiently complete, and selectively segmented. Realistically, grasping the whole of the whole is unlikely at this time, or perhaps ever. What is necessary is that there lies within, sufficient understanding –

adequate seeing of wholeness – to take up the work, to move towards wholeness. A life of the whole perspective, seeing ourselves as part of life, and understanding intent and intended ways of working in that regard, has shown itself to be an effective perspective for going forward... a going forward that itself is inspirited through faith, faith that if we maintain serious intent with regard to the work, we will be given access to necessary seeing and understanding.

Selectively segmented, on the other hand, works to keep us anchored in the current plane of existence... continues to breathe life into that which divides, that which keeps us from moving towards wholeness... and often orients us towards our wish, our image, versus the unfolding image of the Source.

We are, by a partial perspective, creating a shadow that blocks out the light of the Source... not unlike earth during the process of eclipse, casting a shadow on the moon... then our taking that segment which remains visible as representing the whole of the moon... the moon, one moon that we all claim to share. What becomes shadowed away being the whole of the truth of the Source, the whole of the truth of our humanness, the whole of the intent for us to become fully and truly human.

The Unfolding "Think a New Way"

"Think a new way" is a pattern common to upward shifts… a pattern we can see within ourselves, within our lives… and a pattern relevant to upward shifts in our humanness… shifts along the path of intent, the path of our unfolding potential… potential to be and become fully and truly human.

Now is the time of potential. "Think a new way" emerges as coming from a perspective of potential, a life of the whole perspective, a perspective that recognizes our livingness, our membership in life, and the intended ongoingness of life… a perspective necessary for our moving towards wholeness, away from that which divides… and the required perspective for taking up pursuits that work for all children, all children in the world… a perspective that focuses on being and becoming.

It is natural as we awaken and seek to understand and embrace this unfolding "think a new way" that we become more conscious of current ways and focus… a consciousness that brings forth, makes real, the boundaries to cross; and the realities of a step change versus an improvement of what is. Clarity of calling and the work before us emerge as well. And too, at this time, we notice the shift from focusing on human failings to focusing on human potential – in particular, on ways of advancing our humanness.

As we reflect on the unfolding "think a new way," it is helpful to remember that the essential truths of the previous are enfolded into the intended unfolding… emerging as deeper, more wholistic expressions of truth… truth essential to our becoming.

164

The Working of the Unfolding Process of Intent

The essential truths of the previous are enfolded into the unfolding and emerge as higher, deeper, more wholistic expressions of truth... essential truths.

This is the way of working of the unfolding process of intent, a way of working that reflects an upward thrust within and through life... an upward thrust that requires deeper expressions, more wholistic manifestations of truth... an upward thrust that, from time to time, requires a shift, a step change... a shifting, not only in terms of platforms of existence, but also a shift in being... a shift in being that will bring forth a real shift in doing... a shift in being and doing, a more authentic expression of the intent of the Source.

Here again we see faith at work, the nature of faith required to transcend what is, to reach for, to work towards that which is now called for... the becoming that is present within the intended unfolding... in particular the intended unfolding at this time of potential. It is natural for us to hang onto, to cling to, the familiar, the comfortable, that which we have come to know, that which we have put faith in, an attachment that is naturally strengthened and reinforced by culture... the inherent working of culture.

We can see this pattern of enfolding essential truths into intended unfolding through the teachings of Christ with regard to the two commandments. Early in his public works he describes the commandments of *Love God, Love thy neighbor* (MK12:30) as being all-encompassing with regard to the truths of all the commandments and the truths of the prophets; prophets being a process by which truths, new truths, enter into the world of humanity. Later on, he lifts up a new commandment, the going forward commandment

165

of *Love one another as I have loved you* (JN13:34), a commandment made possible for us by his saying "Yes" (LK22:42) to the will of the Father, and his taking up of the work for which he was sent. We can with a bit of reflection, see the essential truth of loving thy neighbor enfolded within the new commandment.

Entering into the Process of Unfolding Work

Work, taking up unfolding work, both unfolds and makes real our potential... unfolding work enables the intended unfolding, not as we would wish, but rather in the image of the Source. Unfolding work is the work that moves us in the direction of being more truly human, of becoming an increasingly authentic instrument of the Source.

Each and all have potential; each has a gift to bring, spirit to manifest... an essential organizing truth for the compassion of equality. We enter into the process of unfolding work through work of the heart, called work that emerges through essence, patterns of intent, patterns of intent that enable the advancing of our humanness... patterns that move us in the direction of congruence with intent, harmony with intended ways of working.

Unfolding work seeks and is guided by wisdom, the wisdom of intent; wisdom, being present to creation, is present to intent and intended ways of working; and is accessible through the intuition of wholeness... wholeness with regard to the whole of life, including the wholeness of humanity.

At this time of potential, community is the smallest whole. The called work, the unfolding work of the one, is encompassed within the essence, essential work of the community; a similar pattern for community and country is beginning to emerge.

Much of our experience of faith – faith related to the here and now – is organized by existence, the realities of existence. Going forward faith moves towards being organized by essence – patterns of intent... patterns that bring a new perspective from which to engage existence... from which to organize ourselves, our systems and processes. All of which brings forth the possibility for a renewal of faith, not so much in what was, but more in what is intended.

"Thy Kingdom Come" as an Expression of Intent

Reflecting on *Thy kingdom come, thy will be done, on earth as in heaven* (MT6:10) as an expression of intent, an intent for the coming of the kingdom, brings forth some thoughts. We see within that expression – the coming of the kingdom – an unfolding with regard to the ways of living, of working and of being that are more and more congruent with intent… a seeing and understanding of intent that becomes possible through a wholistic embracement of the Source, and a life of the whole perspective.

With regard to will, we see…

> Thy Will can, and is necessary for, advancing humanness, fulfilling the intent of the Source.
> My will seeks to improve existence, bring about improvement consistent with my wish, my image.
> Surrendering to Thy will, saying "Yes" to wholistic intent, frees my will to move in the direction of congruence with intent, and harmony with intended ways of working.
> Faith, going forward faith, becomes much more wholistic, particularly with regard to the here and unfolding now – the kingdom coming process – and the hereafter – the process of our returning.

As we reflect and dialogue on faith, it may be useful to remember:
> Neither grace, the grace commonly associated with salvation, nor love, the love essential to becoming, can enter a self-serving heart.
> What is true for the one would seem to be equally true for a community, a country, a people.

Developing a Here and Unfolding Now Faith-Based Culture

Looking further at faith coming from existence, we see that at its core is integrity. We expect integrity within and from those to whom we look for knowledge. We also expect, and require, integrity within the processes essential to our well-being… educating of the children, governing, banking, transporting, etc., integrity within the systems we construct to support and serve essential human/life processes. As integrity diminishes, so too does faith, that which we put faith in. As faith begins to diminish and disappear, we find ourselves on the inevitable path of becoming a faithless people… a people void of faith, and all the obvious consequences of that.

Now is the time of unfolding potential… a time for moving towards wholeness, away from that which divides… a time for taking up pursuits that work for all children, all children in the world… and a time for regenerating the essential ground of human life… a time for developing a here and unfolding now faith-based culture… a culture with sufficient integrity that faith, ableness to put faith in, is a reality… a practiced and experientially validated way of living and working… not only with regards to ourselves, but with regard to the whole of life as well.

Continuing on with our reflection on a here and unfolding now faith-based culture, we begin to see a more wholistic expression of integrity… integrity encapsulated within intentional ethics (It is useful to remember that during times of unfolding, the essence of the truths of the previous are enfolded within the unfolding, emerging as higher order, deeper, more whole expressions of truth).

Intentional Ethics: *The pursuit of right and good, sustaining an aim of congruence with intent, harmony with intended ways of working.* In this context, we can see integrity – which has the character of completeness, of wholeness – upwardly shifting to a life of the whole perspective... a perspective that is fully inclusive of the truths in human centeredness, but uses the larger whole of life for both orientation and direction... our way of being and doing, what we pursue.

What emerges through the development, understanding and practice of intentional ethics is the regeneration of faith, not so much in terms of what was, but rather in terms of what is needed... what is critical and necessary at this time. So now we look to living systems – our own as well as those related to the whole of life – in terms of integrity... of our maintaining ethical integrity with regard to all living systems, with essential life processes... an intent on our part that is greatly enabled by conscientious attention to what works for all children in the world – now and in the unfolding future.

Further thoughts bring forth the Common Law of Earthly Life: *Ultimately, the perspective we hold, where we start our thinking from, determines the path we take, the direction we move in, what we move towards, what we move away from.* We can see in the working of intentional ethics/integrity, guided by a life of the whole perspective, that which truly enables our moving towards wholeness, away from that which divides.

Reflecting further on our current culture brings to mind the common and active start points of legality, economics and rights. We notice the natural diminishment of ethics, ethical pursuits as legality – being safely legal – becomes more and more predominant... engendering a diminished platform and basis for life, for living... one that moves in the direction of decreasing faith. We also notice the potential that becomes possible as rights are enfolded into the unfolding… emerging as pursuing the right and good – right for the whole of humanity and good for the whole of life – intentional ethics. In a similar sort of way, we see economics emerging as wholistic economics, reciprocally nourishing economics anchored in and built around virtue-based values. Thus economics shifts from a start point to that which is necessary to sustain the advancement and realization of virtue.

Finally, we see within intentional ethics, a power not only to halt the current disintegration of faith in our systems, but also the power to bring into being that which is beyond the current – that which reflects the intended unfolding. Laws, at this time of potential, do not disappear; rather they take up their intended work with regard to integrity.

The Emerging Humanizing Mind;
The Minds of Existence and Essence

Mind is an organizing phenomenon, an organizing process around a core of work and purpose. At this time of potential, the particular work and purpose that have come to the fore is that of advancing our humanness and intentional purpose – intentional purpose being purpose that reflects intent and intended ways of working... a central core around which is emerging a humanizing mind... a mind required for advancing our humanness, for taking on intentional purpose... a mind that sees spirit – the accessing and manifesting of spirit – as that which brings significance and completeness to the minds of existence and essence... a significance and completeness that enables a harmonious synergy between the two, such that we can move forward along the path of becoming fully and truly human... a humanizing mind that both reflects our potential to be and become fully and truly human, and makes visible processes for the realization of that potential.. the potential to fulfill the intent of the Source... the mind necessary for taking up the soul building work of moving towards wholeness, away from that which divides... and for taking up pursuits that work for all children, all children in the world... a mind that recognizes that at this time of potential, community is the smallest whole.

Contrasting the minds of existence and essence adds imagery, more seeing, to the emerging humanizing mind. Contrasting versus comparing because through contrasting we can see the beauty and uniqueness of each, not unlike how we might look at two of our children... and hopefully, in this way, we can better see the harmony and synergy that the humanizing mind – through spirit – is working to bring forth... to make real.

173

The mind of existence needs and seeks structure to have meaning. It looks to the perspective of problem, problem-solving, to bring clarity with regard to work and purpose. For the most part, it focuses on function and functioning – in a doing sense. It looks to reason as the means to gain knowledge, factual knowledge... most often knowledge with regard to cause and effect – if this is done, if this occurs, then this will happen, these are the consequences. This pursuit of knowledge, facts, and literal interpretation follows the reductionist path of reason – a path of reducing wholes into parts... more and more parts about which more and more knowledge – fact supported knowledge – can be gained... a process that has high reliance upon and value for memory and the ability to skillfully apply knowledge. It is what we look to with regard to bringing structures into existence, and resolving problems with regard to structures. The mind of existence is commonly at work in such things as science, engineering, theology, traditional philosophy, etc.

The mind of essence looks to process for seeing and under-standing, process related to wholeness and intended ways of working with regard to wholeness. It looks to the perspec-tive of potential with regard to bringing clarity to work and purpose – work and purpose with regard to a larger whole, in particular the larger whole of life. While it does pay attention to – keep in mind so to speak – function and doing, it much more focuses on being – the inner experi-ence of the process of interaction. It looks to the intuition of wholeness for seeing and understanding – for gaining a deeper, more wholistic understanding of truth. It seeks wholeness rather than fractionation, and engages in the processes of reflection and dialogue to generate this. It is what we look to, to see and gain understanding of essence – patterns of intent and intended ways of working. It is an emerging mind, the developing of which is enabled by the

174

living philosophy of potential… an essence-based, versus existence-anchored, philosophy.

Critical to sustaining authenticity and integrity of the humanizing mind is clarity with regard to Source… there is a Source; we are not the source. The humanizing mind actively seeks to resist the all too common temptation of imaging and acting as if we are the source… or that we can through cleverness, smartness, and invention, replace the Source… in effect "make" the Source irrelevant, non-existent. Imaging ourselves as source is an all too common source of false images… false images we have of ourselves… false images that lead us away from advancing our humanness… false images that inevitably take us down a path of diminishing humanness. Also, equally important with regard to authenticity and integrity, is the embracing and the seeking of understanding of intent and intended ways of working.

Lead Us Not into Temptation

Lead us not into temptation is a prayerful notion that I have long struggled with… struggled with in regards to apparent incongruencies with images I have held with regard to the Source… the will force behind the whole of creation.

Some recent contemplations and dialogue has brought forth some imagery and understanding that is providing some satisfaction with regard to my struggle and questioning. I have no doubt that a deeper, more wholistic understanding and imagery will eventually come forth… however, here is what has appeared.

There is a path of potential, a path of intent… a path for seeking congruence with intent, for taking up pursuits that reflect intended ways of working. Virtues are critical guiding elements – true instruments – for our taking up the path of intent; for our becoming, our being intentional people. There is hazard within the working… hazard present within intended unfolding. We experience this hazard through temptation… temptation is ever and always present along the path of intent. Thus when accessing, living from virtue, temptation can and does enter… most commonly in terms of seeking cultural status from and recognition of our "goodness"… and perhaps more seriously, we are tempted to see ourselves as the source.

Recognition, especially recognition of goodness, and the illusion of being the source, are natural inclinations that can become difficult-to-transcend attachments… attachments to energies of existence, energies that occlude the accessing of spirit, the spirit and willfulness present in and along the path of intent.

Temptation comes to us through reason – the instrument of

our doing... temptation works to occlude – block out – wisdom, and to generate the logic and rationale for our pursuits... pursuits that emanate from the illusion of our being the source, having the right to, etc... manifestations of what we commonly refer to as our ego – our self-centeredness... that which ignores intent, intended ways of working... the right and good.

These thoughts have come together in what would be a sort of footnote to the prayer (MT6:9-13) that contains *Lead us not into temptation*:

Lead us not into temptation... as we strive to live in ways congruent with intent,

Give us the strength to resist the cultural pulls – that which takes us off and away from the path of intent...

Help us to not succumb to the natural inclinations of recognition and illusions of our being the source...

Help us to be organized by Thy will...

Lead us away from having and pursuing motives and motivations that come from existence...

Rescue us from self-centered intent...

Keep us firmly on the path of Thy will, away from the path of my will temptations.

Finally, this writing has brought new and deeper insight to an old saying of my father: "The road to hell is paved with good intentions."

Closing Thoughts…

GOING FORWARD…
SAYING "YES"

To be Clear…

To be clear, these writings, these reflections, the ongoing intentional dialoguing are all about – of and from – philosophy. Whereas, given the nature of the work before us, some of the subject matter dealt with is common to theology/religion; this is not theology – reasoned interpretation of the word; rather, this is about a particular philosophy – a life of the whole, essence-based philosophy…

A philosophy referred to as the living philosophy of potential.

A philosophy anchored in Source: One Source, all else instruments; and emanating from and through the Source is intent and intended ways of working within and through life – the ongoing, intentional, upward unfolding of life on and through earth.

A philosophy that focuses on becoming, on realizing our potential to become fully and truly human… which in turn requires of us the taking on of a life of the whole perspective, a perspective that both transcends the limitations of, and fully embraces the truths within our current human centered perspective.

And ultimately, a philosophy aimed at enabling our returning to following a path of intent, a path sourced in original intent, an unfolding intentional path of life… a way of being and becoming an intentional people.

Through the development and processing of this philosophy, some seeing and understandings have emerged that are critical to now – to the work of now. To begin with: The perspective we hold, where we start our thinking from, determines the path we take, the direction we move in, what we move towards, what we move away from. Thus the significance of the shift from human centered to a life of the whole centered perspective, a perspective that allows us to see ourselves, and especially all our children, as woven within the processes of life… not environmentally, ecologically separated from, but fully and truly woven within the unfolding intentional processes of life. And to see ourselves having, like all of life's members, work and role with regard to the sustaining and ongoingness of life, the eternalizing of life on and through the earth: to act in accord with Thy will… to live in accord with *the Father's command of eternal life – on earth as in heaven* (Jn12:50; Mt6:10).

Real shifts, upward shifts, involve – call upon – both heart and mind, not as separate phenomenon, but rather as systemic expressions of the whole… the whole of the work before us, the whole of the work now called for along the path of intent, the path of our potential… the whole reflected in opening our hearts to the mother's command, *Work for all my children in the world*… the whole reflected in developing the mind – the seeing and understanding – required for bringing the world of our making into congruence with the world of intent… and the wholeness of heart and mind that enables our moving towards wholeness, away from that which divides.

A necessary reality of our entering into life on earth is the development of a world view – a view of the world that encompasses both the visible and the invisible aspects of our world. How we see the world greatly influences our thoughts and actions regarding philosophy, science and religion; all of which in turn greatly influence our culture – the development and ways of our culture. How we process the visible and invisible aspects of our world is grounded in our perspective and directionally organized by mind – the particular mind of the time. A human centered perspective naturally brings with it the urges of instinct – survival, procreation, etc., of the species – and the application of intellect, the development of intelligence for personal, human advantage. The dominant mind has been the reasoning mind of existence... dealing with both the visible and the invisible through reasoned interpretation, seeking structure to have meaning, and pursuing segmentation and reductionism to become knowledgeable – expert, an authoritative source in particular arenas. All of which seek to serve humanity both in terms of existence – our having a good life – and in terms of afterlife – the invisible segment of life.

Now... at this time... given the children's reality – the reality and obvious direction of the world of our making – and the work before us, we are being called upon to access and develop the intuitive mind of essence... to see and come from essence – patterns of intent – versus starting our thinking from existential structures... to orient ourselves to realizing potential versus segmented problem solving. A reality and work requiring the seeing of process, the seeking of wholeness... the nature of directional organizing now required, a directional organizing not possible through the reasoning mind of existence acting in and of itself; but one which requires the reasoning mind of existence to carry out, to be manifested in the world of our making. A directional organizing that brings forth a yin and yang complementarity between the intuitive mind of essence and the reasoning mind of existence... providing of course that the yin of intuition and the yang of reason come from, share in, and are disciplined about the truths of Source:

One Source, all else instruments...

Emanating from and through the Source is intent and

185

*intended ways of working of life and of ourselves
within life…*

A wholeness within, a systemic way of working, which makes possible – moves us in the direction of – becoming intentional people: a people with hearts open to all children in the world, a people developing and processing a world view through a wholistic mind of intent – an intentional systemic harmonious working of intuition and reason.

Finally, on the path of intent, the initiating process of our returning to the path of intent is the repotentializing of ethics, in particular, intentional ethics, ethics sourced in the intentional ways of life. To contemplate, to dialogue, the subject of ethics requires some consideration of morality – the complementary companion of ethics. In one sort of way we can see morality in terms of consequences – not only within the present human community, but also within the context of afterlife, and associated with that, the notions of salvation, being saved, sinfulness, forgiveness, etc. On the other hand, intentional ethics deal with the ongoingness, the eternalizing of life on and through the earth, and the willfulness on our part to not only not interfere with, but rather nourish and honor life's systems and processes, nourish and honor intent and intended ways of working of life – the whole of life… a willfulness that reflects our commitment to see and understand intent – to start our thinking from that versus gaining manipulative knowledge for bringing about that which reflects our will, our desire. Associated with intentional ethics is not so much the notion of forgiveness, of wiping the slate clean; but rather the notion of redemption, of our returning to the path of intent… returning and taking up our work and role in the ongoingness of life… our moving towards nourishing life, towards realizing potential… our moving away from self-centered extraction.

186

The living philosophy of potential is all about life... the here and unfolding now... and about work... work as the means to manifest spirit, the accessing and manifesting of spirit, spirit essential to the eternalizing of life... work requiring we see life as process, see Christ as process... and work requiring the process of intentional dialoguing. All of which begins (or not) with the development of serious intent...

From the perspective of the living philosophy of potential, earth, life and our entry into earthly life came about through serious intent of the Source.

We, being unique among life's creatures, were created in the image and likeness of the Source... and thus have the inherent capacity to take on and come from serious intent.

Through serious intent we can transcend ordinary life limitation and become fully and truly human... true instruments of the Source.

The Unfolded Work before Us

Ultimately...
our moving towards wholeness, away from that
which divides,
our taking up pursuits that work for all children
in the world,
is limited by our ableness to fully embrace the wholeness
of Source... the wholeness manifested in our being living
human beings, people of earth, members in the larger
community of life.

We cannot move towards wholeness, nor pursue that
which works for all, with a partial perspective.

All the work that has gone on before, that which we have embraced and participated in, has the character of preparation... preparation for that which is before us... the unfolded work before us... the authentic taking up of the work of that which works for all children in the world... work that requires an intentional life of the whole perspective... the embracing of the truth of our livingness, of our being of and from the Source of life – the living Source, the Source of love, truth and good... work that requires the transcending of the limitations of a human centered perspective, limitations that interfere with our becoming fully and truly human.

An image of the work, a working image, of that which embraces the work, is beginning to emerge. It has the character of yin and yang... a more wholistic expression than I have previously seen... a more clear seeing of the sphere – the whole – which needs to be present for the yin and the yang to actually be... to work as intended. The whole being the mind, the mind of the intuition of wholeness, the particular expression called for... the mind that embraces the essential truths of the minds of existence and essence... the emerging advancing humanness mind of now... the mind that enables the minds of existence and essence to shift from polarity to synchronicity. It is the mind that enables us to see *it is really all about life.*

We can see that flowing out from the heart of the mind of existence is "the seeking of eternal life"... the central aim, wish and work of the mind of existence... a human centered perspective.

We can see that flowing out from the heart of the mind of essence is "the joining in the process of eternalizing life"... the central aim, wish and work of the mind of essence... a life of the whole centered perspective.

We can see that flowing out from the heart of the emerging advancing humanness mind is "the becoming intentional people of life"... the central aim, wish and work of the emerging mind of advancing humanness... an intentional living human being perspective.

Seeing the minds of existence and essence being embraced by – enfolded within – the emerging advancing humanness mind; and through that process, the forming of the yin and yang relatedness between the two; is useful directional imagery for this work – the unfolded work before us... the work, the work for all children in the world... the central core of all work at this time.

Out from the unfolding work will emerge processes for creating communities that come from a life of the whole perspective... and processes for authentically taking up pursuits that work for all children in the world... pursuits that bring the world of our making into congruence with intended ways of working of life on this earth.

Intentionally Working Love

Intentionally working love…

*Love entering into the working of the world through essence…
manifesting as compassion… bringing forth the particular organizing required for the unfolding work – the particular advancing
being called for.*

The particular advancing being called for…

> *Becoming a vessel for love entering… becoming an
> instrument for intended unfolding…*
>> *is the way, our way, of loving the Source…*

> *Seeking to come from essence… enabling the discovering
> of essence and the accessing and manifesting of spirit…
> joining in the unfolding work…*
>> *is the way, our way, of loving one another.*

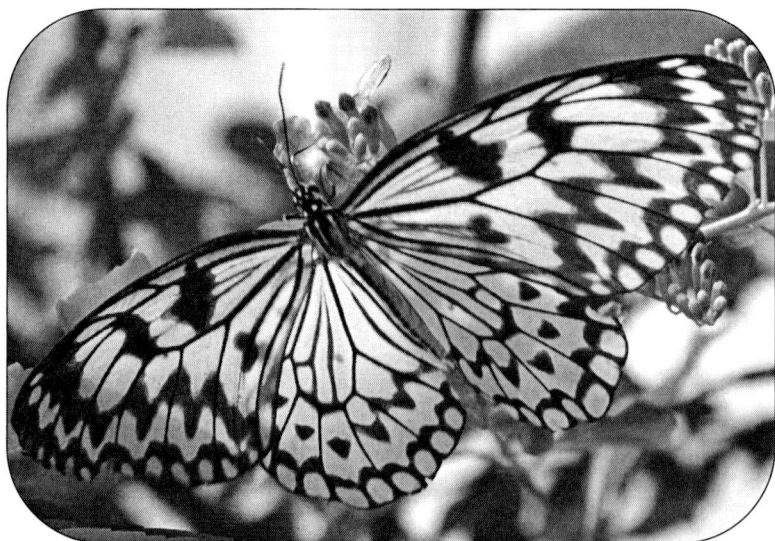